UNWIN UNIVERSITY BOOKS

I I

THE PRINCIPLES OF
ECONOMIC PLANNING

W. ARTHUR LEWIS

THE PRINCIPLES OF
ECONOMIC PLANNING

A study prepared for the
Fabian Society

NEW EDITION
WITH A NEW INTRODUCTION

LONDON
UNWIN UNIVERSITY BOOKS

FIRST PUBLISHED IN GREAT BRITAIN IN 1949
BY DENNIS DOBSON LTD., ST. JAMES'S, LONDON, S.W.1
AND GEORGE ALLEN AND UNWIN LTD., MUSEUM STREET,
LONDON, W.C.1

Second Impression 1950
Second Edition 1952
Second Impression 1954
Third Impression 1956
Fourth Impression 1959
Fifth Impression 1961
Sixth Impression 1963
Seventh Impression 1965
Eighth Impression 1968
Third Edition 1969

SBN 04 330137 1

UNWIN UNIVERSITY BOOKS

George Allen & Unwin Ltd.
40 *Museum Street, London, W.C.*1

PRINTED IN GREAT BRITAIN
BY COMPTON PRINTING LTD.
LONDON AND AYLESBURY

INTRODUCTION TO THE THIRD EDITION

THIS book was originally published without a Preface. The reason for this is that it was never meant to be a book. The Fabian Society asked me in July 1948 for a pamphlet on the economic perplexities of contemporary Britain, and this was what I set out to write. Unfortunately, the perplexities were so numerous that the pamphlet turned up at 120 pages, instead of the usual thirty. So it was put between hard covers.

Thus the book is not, as its title might suggest, an academic study of theoretical principles, but is rather a political statement. Neither does it cover the whole field of planning, but concentrates rather on some topics which happened to be of special interest in Great Britain in the summer of 1948. Perhaps it was wrongly named. It should have been called 'A Brief Statement on Some Current Topics in British Planning'; but it is too late to change its name.

A book is like a child; it has a separate existence and a career of its own, which its author only barely understands. I thought I had written an ephemeral pamphlet, which might last six months and be read by perhaps a thousand members of the British Labour Party. Instead, it came to be translated into several languages, European and Asian, and finds about as many new readers today (1968) as it did in its first year. It seems clear that many countries, on every continent, have had and still have problems not too different from those of Britain in 1948. So my audience was wider than I had thought.

Inevitably the focus of British problems has changed in the course of twenty years; some seem less important now than they did then (e.g. the role of licensing), while others (e.g. the conditions for technological pre-eminence) interest the public much more now than they did then. So the balance of topics in the book could not be the same if one were writing it today.

This is not the kind of book that one can rewrite twenty years later without spoiling its flavour, so I have decided to leave it as it was first published. New readers, however, deserve some sort of up-dating, so this Preface has been written to take some account of the passage of time. It is only a brief guide to shifts in public interest, so the reader must not expect extended treatment of new issues.

II

The pamphlet was primarily concerned with two of the problems then bothering contemporary social democrats. First, what are the essentials of socialism? The inheritance of British socialists in 1948 included four separate ideas, namely political democracy, the class-

I

less society, nationalisation and planning. It is possible to believe in any one of these four while rejecting the other three. The position taken in the first chapter of the book was that the first two are the essential ideas of social democracy. These are ends, whereas the other two, nationalisation and planning, are only means, which have both advantages and disadvantages, and are more relevant in some situations than in others. One could not be a social democrat if one did not believe in democracy and the classless society, but social democrats could reasonably differ among themselves about the extent and kinds of nationalisation and planning which were appropriate to different circumstances.

The rest of the book was about economic planning, defined for this purpose as government action designed to secure results different from those of the market. The book reviews the weaknesses of the market, and considers the type of action appropriate to each problem. Types of planning are classified as persuasion, direction, and inducement. The book argues for inducement as the principal weapon (subsidies, taxes, loans), with direction (licenses, quotas) used only sparingly and temporarily. Beyond this the book argues that the chief function of planning is to get the general framework of economic activity right, and in particular to ensure full employment, high savings rates, and realistic foreign exchange rates.

Nowadays these propositions seem rather commonplace, but they were not so in 1948. In the first place, the most powerful self-styled socialist of the day was Josef Stalin, still admired throughout the world as the hero of a victorious war, and not yet discredited by his aggressions in Eastern Europe or by Khrushchev's later "revelations". Stalin believed neither in democracy nor in economic equality; his emphasis was on public ownership and planning. Under the shadow of this powerful personality most of the world's socialists were not a little confused. And in the second place, the world had just emerged from a great war, which is a situation that de-emphasises democracy and elevates government control of resources. It was natural for socialists to carry some of this thinking over into the post-war years. With the passage of time these influences have been eroded, and most social democrats now have little difficulty in distinguishing between ends and means.

The failure of Stalinism in the Communist countries themselves has also made a profound impression. A century ago Marx and Bakunin battled for the mind of the trade union movement, Bakunin arguing the philosophy of anarchism, which implies decentralisation and local participatory democracy, while Marx argued for the highly centralised state, if only as a temporary step towards the freer world to come. Marx defeated Bakunin, and the socialist movement drifted towards identification with the all-powerful state. Now in the post-Stalinist era ordinary men are rejecting Marx everywhere, and turning towards Bakunin. From their point of view working for the big communist or nationalised trust is indistinguishable from working for the large capitalist corporation; the bosses may be chosen differently, but the bossing is the same. We have moved into an era where the ordinary man has been coming out into the streets against "the establishment", whatever its political colour, and demanding the right to participate in making the social decisions which control his life. The movement has passed beyond the factories and workshops; the students are protesting; minorities (Scottish, Walloon and others) are demanding self-determination; federations are breaking up; even the Catholic Church is having to decentralise. Socialism must base itself on a minimum of centralised powers, or it will not hold the allegiance of new generations.

This yearning for "grass roots democracy" has profound consequences with which most socialist planners have not yet come to grips. It means that units of control must be kept as small as possible. It affects decisions about the appropriate extent of nationalisation, when compared with other measures for redistributing property. Within the sphere of public property it raises such questions as the structure of industry (e.g. the number of competing public corporations), of the combination of private management with public property (of which more later) and of the appropriate relations between consumers, workers, managers and central planners. It can no longer be taken for granted, as so many socialists thought during the first half of the 20th century, that socialism must identify itself with the powerful central state. On the contrary, if socialism is to survive in the second half of the 20th century it must now deliberately learn as much from Bakunin's objectives (not his methods) as it did from Marx.

Another new factor which has forced socialists to re-think their programmes from top to bottom, using the distinction between ends and means, has been the need to come to grips with the requirements for economic growth. Early socialist writing says nothing about economic growth; the societies described are most often static; and the problem is only how to divide up the economic pie. Karl Marx recognised the importance of growth, but took it for granted that the problem had been solved; invest more capital, and output would automatically grow. By the time that socialist parties began to come into power, between the two world wars, the problem was not how to ensure growth but how to prevent decline, since unemployment was the biggest problem of the times. Securing a per capita increase of 2 to 4 per cent per annum was not elevated into a national objective in the countries of Western Europe until after the second world war.

To integrate economic growth into socialist thought is to impose severe constraints on the imagination, since socialists have imagined many kinds of ideal societies which are obviously inconsistent with economic growth. For example, economic growth requires incentives; it is therefore not consistent with absolutely equal pay, or with "to each according to his need"; and it is helped by rewarding managers in accordance with the profits and losses resulting from their work—all of which the Russian socialists now fully recognise.

Again, economic growth requires saving and is therefore not consistent with paying the worker "the whole produce of his labour". Economic growth requires successful competition in world markets, and so the ratio between the internal and external values of the currency is crucial; this plays no part in socialist doctrine, but has its consequences for other matters which do, such as the role of the trade unions, the efficiency of different kinds of business organisation, or the respective roles of fiscal and monetary policy. If economic growth is ignored, any philosopher or dreamer can write a treatise describing his ideal society, and many have done so. But if the socialist society is to incorporate 2 or 3 per cent per capita growth per annum, and be both democratic and classless, the blueprint needs some pretty expert drafting! It is no accident that British Labour governments, reared on the socialist theories of the first half of the 19th century, have always been brought down by their inability to cope with the economic crises of the twentieth.

In this Preface I shall consider briefly how social democratic thinking has evolved over the past twenty years with respect to the two points on which this book turned: that socialism should use the market, and that its touchstone is equality.

III

Let us begin with planning. The new emphasis on long-run economic growth has stimulated the making of economic plans for several years ahead—five, ten, fifteen or even twenty. Some partial long-range planning there has always been, whether in the public sector (of roads, electric power, universities) or in the private sector (investment programmes of individual corporations). The new phenomenon is the making by the government (with more or less collaboration from private enterprise) of a "plan" for the whole economy, public and private.

The U.S.S.R. has been making comprehensive plans for the whole economy ever since 1929, but the "plans" now made in Western Europe differ both in detail and in intent. The Soviet Union is a "command" economy. This means that if the plan specifies that x million tons of nails are to be produced in 1968, an order goes out from the government to each factory making nails telling it how many tons of nails are its quota, how many employees it may have, from whom it shall buy iron, and to whom it shall sell the nails. The Western European plans do not go down to factory level; the total is not broken up into units, and no factory manager receives instructions. The plan merely indicates what the planners consider to be feasible. So the process has come to be called "indicative" planning. Obviously the correct word for the operation is not "planning" but "forecasting".

What useful purpose does this forecasting serve? One purpose is beyond dispute. As we have noted, private and public agencies have to make their own long-range plans; everybody making an investment is acting on his long-range plan. The success of each plan depends on the others; whether the plans of those who make steel for sale will be realised over the next twenty years depends partly on the plans now being made by the agencies which will be buying steel over the next twenty years. "Indicative" planning supplies each decision maker with the central planners' view of what may happen to the economy as a whole, if plans are consistent. If the planners have done their job efficiently, in consultation with the large public and private decision makers, their view of the future must help each individual agency, private or public, to improve its own forecasts.

Implicit in this analysis is the possibility that the net effect of publishing an "indicative" plan may be to alter the total of private investment, either upwards, by showing that the economy can grow more rapidly than most investors were expecting, or downwards by showing up obstacles to growth. The indicative planners of the 1950s were mostly men who had matured in the 1920s and 1930s, when private investment was low. They therefore hoped that indicative planning would raise private investment, by showing greater growth potential than private business expected. In the event private business needed no such spur in most of Western Europe in the 1950s. With the notable exception of Great Britain, most of these economies grew faster than their planners had expected, though the record for this is held by Japan, where during the 1950s the rate of growth was consistently 50 to 100 per cent higher than the "plan" had forecast. "Indicative" planning has therefore not yet had much chance to show how it could affect favourably the level of private investment, in times when investment would otherwise be sluggish.

The planners' lack of success in forecasting has helped to discredit another use to which their forecast might have been put. Following the Russian model, the forecasts might have been used as a basis for issuing a quota to each factory. The case for and against this use was much debated at the end of the 1940s; this book was a part of that debate. The battle was already won in Western Europe in the early 1950s. In the early 1960s the Russian economists and administrators began their own battle on the same issue—to de-emphasize quotas and commands, and return their enterprises to control by the market. Nowadays, no social democrat who keeps up with what is going on in Russia assumes any more that licensing is inherently superior to a market mechanism; unless he still hankers after the belief that Stalin could do no wrong.

Clearer analysis of the high rate of growth of industrial production in the U.S.S.R. emphasises that it was due not primarily to centralised planning, but to the very high rates of taxation (including profits) which kept private consumption down to about 60 per cent of the national output. The other 40 per cent was used by the government, *inter alia*, for physical and human capital formation, i.e. for building factories and for a vast programme of education and training. A government must, of course, have a plan for its own expenditures, but this plan does not have to include detailed instructions to each enterprise as to its inputs and outputs. Any economy can have rapid growth whose government, through taxation or otherwise, becomes a source of finance for large programmes of investment in productive assets and in education.

Most of the governments of Western Europe have learnt this lesson. They have tax systems which are so highly progressive that, without any change in tax rates, tax revenue rises faster than national income. They have not therefore been embarrassed for finance, except at times when they have thought it necessary sharply to increase their military budgets. Subject to this military constraint, it has been possible to spend lavishly on education and housing, and where necessary to make sums available to private investment through public financial agencies. (In this respect they contrast markedly with governments in the less developed world, whose inadequate fiscal structures generally result in government revenues rising more slowly than national product).

Thanks to the buoyancy of both private investment and public expenditure, Western European growth rates have been unprecedently high; but two nagging problems remain, the cyclical fluctuation, and the tendency to rising prices, with which is associated trouble in the balance of payments.

Following the lead of Lord Keynes it was confidently expected at the end of the 1940s that cyclical fluctuations could be eliminated by a combination of good forecasting with appropriate financial weapons. The trade cycle has not proved to be much of a problem, but insofar as it has operated, experience in controlling it is not spectacular.

The trade cycle is not much of a problem in periods when the economy is moving upwards on a prolonged upswing (e.g. 1850-75 in the U.K., 1895-1913 in the U.S.A.). Downturns occur, but they are short and mild. The world economy has been in one of its periods of prolonged upswing ever since the end of the second world war, so Keynesian tools have not been put to a serious test.

This is fortunate, since the difficulties have made themselves quite obvious. The first is that of making correct forecasts of how the economy is going to behave over the next twelve months. Economic forecasting is not now significantly ahead of weather forecasting. The technique has improved immensely over the past twenty years, partly because the statistics at our disposal increase every day, and partly because the electronic computer now makes it much easier to handle complicated relationships than was possible twenty years ago. However, the future remains (and will always remain) unpredictable. One has to act on the best information one has, but it will frequently let one down.

The other difficulty is that the weapons for controlling the cycle are blunt. Twenty years ago the fiscal weapon was emphasised. The government was to lower taxes (or increase expenditure) if it forecast deflation; or to raise taxes (reduce expenditure) if it forecast inflation.

Perfection here demands a degree of flexibility which a democratic government does not possess; people and Parliament co-operate with it when it proposes to cut taxes or increase expenditure, but they resist when the situation demands the opposite remedies. Partly for these reasons the monetary weapon now tends to receive greater emphasis; the central bank can raise (or reduce) interest rates overnight, without consulting Parliament, and such action will discourage (or stimulate) certain kinds of business investment. This, however, is also a blunt tool, since changes in interest rates have a wide range of effects (e.g. changes in capital values) beyond the immediate intention of stimulating or checking business investment for the next year or two.

The reader will find these difficulties mentioned in Chapters III and IV of this book, but he will also see that they are not emphasised. Economists are as confident today as they were in 1948 that the government can prevent the economy from experiencing a major depression, which was what we all then feared. But it is also clear that not all Parliaments are as yet willing to grant their governments all the flexibility which is needed to cope with minor fluctuations. Nowhere is this more obvious than in the United States of America in 1967-68.

The other problem, that of controlling prices, is fully emphasised in Chapters III and V. Its seriousness has not diminished especially in Great Britain.

The British economy is heavily dependent on imports of food and raw materials. It is inevitable that if the economy grows swiftly its imports of raw materials will also grow swiftly. In this respect its position is worse today than it was forty years ago, when the basic materials were coal and iron ore, which it possessed. Now they are oil and the light metals which Britain does not possess. So when the economy grows swiftly imports grow swiftly, and the economy can be kept in balance only by having an equally swift growth of exports. British export prices must therefore be strictly competitive with those of other industrial countries.

Britain has been weak at two points. First, wages have risen consistently faster than productivity, to the extent that British prices have been rising faster than those of other industrial nations. This alone makes devaluation inevitable from time to time, if it continues. The situation has not changed in this respect since 1948, except that it is now more widely understood inside the trade union movement.

The other weak point is the loss of technological leadership. If in addition to importing food and raw materials Britain has to import the new capital goods (jet planes, computers, machine tools) a burden is placed on exporters which they can hardly bear—that of achieving a high and rising level of exports of old-time commodities. An economy so dependent on foreign trade can have a high wage level only if it is in the forefront of technical change. The British have been conscious for half a century of their technological backwardness, but did not come to grips with it until the end of the second world war. They then launched a programme which began with visits of workers and employers to American factories, and went on with Development Councils, new laws against monopoly, subsidies to industrial research, and a new attitude to education (including technological and managerial education). The biggest change of recent years is the new emphasis on education. If one compares Britain with the United States, the top 5 per cent and the bottom 60 per cent are about equally educated, but those in the 6th to 40th percentiles are much better educated in the U.S.A. than in Britain. This may be the reason why, while the Americans are no more fertile than the British (per 1,000 of population) in coming up with new fundamental ideas, the Americans seem to be much better than the British in developing new techniques. (It is hard to realise now that in 1950 the best jet aeroplane, the Comet, and the best electronic computer, the Ferranti, were British). In this sense the prime cause of British technological backwardness has been the hostility to mass education which is inherent in its class structure.

Given technological backwardness, the economy cannot bear the rate of increase of real wages and prices which the people have sought to enjoy. The British "indicative plan" for 1965-70 has had to be set aside because years of accumulated failure to deal with the wage-price-exchange-rate problem came to a head in 1964, and the absurd attempt to solve the problem by reducing production (1964-7) was inconsistent with the plan's projected growth rate (as well as with commonsense). This does not, however, prove the uselessness of such a plan. On the contrary, the very process of making such a forecast highlights the obstacles to growth—including a too high propensity to import, technological backwardness, slow growth of exports, etc. Provided that everybody remembers that it is impossible to predict the future, indicative planning is a useful framework for putting the problems of growth into a balanced perspective. One learns just as much whether the economy behaves as forecast or not, since honest examination of the reasons for divergence will throw as much light on the weaknesses of the economy as on the weaknesses of forecasting.

IV

The pamphlet's other main thesis was that in socialism equality is the end and nationalisation is only a means. It was pointed out that nationalisation does little for equality, or for industrial peace. Thus socialists could consider each act of nationalisation on its merits, without excessive emotional involvement.

This opinion is not yet shared by all social democrats, but it is held by the overwhelming majority of social democrats in Western Europe. The chapter dealing with this subject needs less revision than any other.

The book makes the point that the essential socialist target is not the income derived from work, but the income derived from

VIII

property. All the socialist schemes—whether progressive taxation, death duties, nationalisation with compensation, or expropriation without compensation—have been aimed at correcting the unequal distribution of income and power which is associated with the unequal distribution of property.

In recent years recognition of economic growth has made possible a new approach to this problem. In an economy which grows by 4 per cent per annum, the amount of man-made capital doubles in about 18 years, and quadruples in about 36 years. If all new capital were public capital, the private (man-made) capital in such an economy would in 36 years be reduced from about 60 to only about 15 per cent of the whole. Therefore even if all existing capital remained in private hands, within 36 years private man-made capital would be a negligible part of the whole. Why then make an enormous fuss to get hold of existing private capital, when by concentrating on making new capital public one could soon reduce private capital to insignificance? This is the first stage of the argument.

The second stage starts from the fact that new capital comes out of new saving. Hence the way to have new capital financed on public rather than private account is to have public saving instead of private saving. Public saving is the difference between the government's revenues and its expenditures on current account (including public enterprises). The essence of this strategy would be to make taxation (and the profits of public enterprise) so heavy that private saving falls and public saving increases. Obviously the only way one can "build a socialist state" i.e. create new capital on public account, is to have a budget surplus (defined to include public profits) large enough to finance capital formation. One cannot "build a socialist state" by borrowing from the private sector to finance capital formation in the public sector, since this means that every bit of new public capital is matched by an equal bit of private wealth in the form of government debt; the government has control over the property, but private wealth continues to grow, and this is not socialism. The strategy of taxing the rich to finance the public sector instead of borrowing the money for them ensures that private wealth shall not grow *pasi passu* with public ownership.

This approach to the problem has its roots in early nineteenth century socialism, which assumed that most saving came out of profits, and that profit was merely a kind of robbery which capitalists performed by selling goods at prices exceeding their cost of production. If profits are merely a private tax which capitalists impose on the public, then it is foolish for the government to borrow from private savings (profits) instead of taxing the same sum away. The modern economist's reformulation of profits as the "earnings" of capital, based on its marginal productivity, makes no moral difference to the argument. More relevant is the question how enterprises would behave if more of their profits were taxed away; this we shall come to in a moment. Also relevant is the fact that there are many economies where corporate profits are still only a small part (5 per cent or less) of national income. In such economies the taxes used to create a large budget surplus would mainly fall on non-profit incomes; partly on rents, and partly on earnings from work.

Now suppose that a socialist government were to adopt this strategy, and instead of (or as well as) emphasising attacks on existing private property, concentrated on effecting a steady increase in the ratio of public saving to national income; what would it do with all this saving? Obviously in the first place it would use it to finance infrastructure; its normal capital programme would be financed by taxing instead of by borrowing. The rest would finance productive industry, whether in the public or in the private sector.

It would be easy to use public funds to finance the private sector. In the first place such funds as accrued in cash could be lent to the private sector, through public development banks, home mortgage associations, agricultural credit agencies, etc.; or could be used to purchase shares. And in the second place, the savings need not accrue in cash. Private corporations retain about a half of their profits for reinvestment in their business. The government could say "in addition to what you now pay as taxes you must assign to us in your books another 20 per cent of your profits which we shall never withdraw in cash, but for which you must issue us ordinary shares". The amount of finance thus available to the management remains the same. The value of the shares held by private shareholders does not rise as much as it would have if all the retained profits were attributed to the private shareholders, but insofar as the management can be distinguished from the shareholders, this does not affect the conduct of the business.

This separation between management and ownership, which is such a feature of the modern large corporation, is also one of the new facts incorporated into modern socialism. For one can now devise schemes combining public ownership with private management. The government can own shares in private corporations, and behave like a private shareholder. The profits thus accrue to the government, rather than to private fortunes, while the advantages of private management are retained.

The separation between management and ownership applies only to large scale enterprises, but this does not matter since few social democrats are concerned about small scale enterprises. In relation to large enterprise, this separation offers a choice of four combinations:

1. Private management of privately owned assets
2. Public   ,,   privately ,,   ,,
3. Private   ,,   publicly   ,,   ,,
4. Public   ,,   publicly   ,,   ,,

No. 1 is private capitalism. No. 2 is nationalisation, as practised by the British Labour Party. The assets belong to the public, in the legal sense, but they are matched by an equal amount of private wealth, since the original assets are acquired by paying compensation, and new assets are financed by borrowing from the private sector. There is wide disillusionment with this system among Western socialists. It has not made the rich any less rich; or solved the problem of industrial peace; or (because of its monopoly element), been particularly amenable to consumer control. So social democratic programmes no longer make nationalisation their big issue.

Mr. Hugh Gaitskell, the leader of the British Labour Party in the latter half of the 1950s was advocating No. 3 just before he died. He saw the virtues of private management, especially in the area of industrial production, where Britain depends on new research and on the development of new commodities and new technologies. He was willing to pursue the strategy of having a large budget surplus, part of which would finance private management. Most of his supporters did not understand the arguments which led up to this proposal, and he was denounced for not emphasizing nationalisation. On the other hand members of the Conservative Party recognised at once that the strategy of building up the budget surplus is more socialist than mere nationalisation, since it checks the growth of private wealth, so he was denounced equally vigorously from the right.

Nevertheless, as disillusionment with nationalisation continues to spread, social democrats must either move backwards to No. 1, as many have done, or more forwards to Nos. 3 or 4, the choice between these two depending largely on the quality of public management. Social democrats in under-developed countries do not have much choice. Since private saving is small, their countries cannot grow rapidly if they depend only on domestic private saving, and they cannot be economically independent if they depend mainly on foreign capital. Hence rapid, independent growth is impossible without large public saving. At the same time, since public administration is weak in their countries, their governments are in no position to run public enterprises honestly and efficiently. So the social democrat in an under-developed country is driven to opt for No. 3, public ownership with private management. This is not a policy that one can adopt overnight, since it is not possible to start running a large budget surplus overnight. It goes without saying that democracy and a revolutionary rate of change are mutually incompatible. And this pamphlet is confined to the problems of social democrats.

Whether one chooses No. 3 or No. 4, the emphasis is on creating publicly owned assets out of public saving. The growth of private wealth is thereby diminished. So when the needs of economic growth (i.e. saving) are incorporated into socialism (i.e. no growth of private wealth), *the essential socialist attitude to property is that there should be a large budget surplus for financing new capital formation in large scale production.*

Leaders of modern socialist thought, like Mr Gaitskell, have grasped this point, but it involves a shift in social democratic attitudes to the budget which is still a long way off. Left-of-centre politics has always viewed the budget as a weapon for transferring income from the rich to the poor, mainly through social services. Hence left-of-centre politicians are perpetually thinking up new ways of increasing public expenditure. But if the central purpose of the budget comes to be, instead, to create a large budget surplus, this can be achieved only by restraining public expenditure. Left-of-centre politicians have to go into reverse, and to start thinking of ways of keeping current expenditure down. This is already beginning to happen. For example, some social democrats are abandoning the principle that the social services must be universal; e.g. that if the poor receive family allowances, so also must the rich. They now speak of excluding people above certain incomes from free enjoyment of the social services.

Another corollary is a change of attitude towards the pricing policies of public enterprise. If profit is merely a robbery of the consumer or the worker, then public enterprises should make no profit; they should just break even. But if profit is a major source of saving, it is highly desirable that public enterprises make profits for use, as public saving, in financing new capital formation. The result of the alternative policy, where public enterprises make no profits, is that every extension of the public sector relatively to the private reduces the economy's propensity to save. This is clearly one reason why the British propensity to save is lower now than it was 60 years ago. It is also a bugbear of less developed countries, whose propensity to run state enterprises at an enormous loss is a drain on their budgets and on national savings. Modern socialists are beginning to argue that nationalised industries should make as much profit as private industries; this comes as a shock to old-fashioned socialists, who expected nationalisation to "reduce exploitation".

Thus, in order to integrate economic growth with socialism, social democrats are being forced to rethink many ideas which they have inherited from the 19th century, with respect to such matters as nationalisation, the social services and budgetary policy. (Conservatives are in the same situation, since the growth of the large corporation, divorcing ownership from management, and incentives from property, has played havoc with some of their age-old arguments). Naturally changes of this magnitude are difficult to effect in the thinking of large masses of people. Socialist doctrine is bound to be in a ferment for the next decade or two, as the leaders re-examine old dogmas, in the light of the distinction between ends and means, and try amid much shouting and confusion, to drag their reluctant followers into the second half of the 20th century.

W.A.L.

Princeton
April, 1968

CONTENTS

I

Why Plan?

THE dispute between planning and *laisser-faire* is not a dispute between order and anarchy in economic life. All serious political thinkers, and not least the *laisser-faire* philosophers, start with the proposition that production and distribution must be controlled to the service of social ends. The point at issue is simply how much of this control may be invisible, and how much must be visible. The invisible control, extolled by the *laisser-faire* protagonists, is that which the market exercises; the visible control, favoured by the planners, is that which is organised by the state.

The control exercised by the market is none the less real and powerful because it is invisible. In a free economy production is controlled by demand. Capitalists cannot produce what they like; self-interest drives them to produce what they can sell, and that is determined by what people demand, and by how much they demand of it. Production for profit is thus, by 'the invisible hand', transmuted into production for use. By the same agency the distribution of income is controlled. Producers cannot charge what they like, for the forces of competition are ever driving prices down to the level of costs, and for ever driving capitalists to improve their efficiency. The free market is thus a powerful instrument of social control, which directs production to the service of demand, stimulates progress, and eliminates excessive earnings.

The case against the invisible control, in favour of state control, cannot proceed by way of blank denial. It is obvious that the invisible hand exists, and that its influence is beneficial. Neither can the case be founded, as some suppose, on attacking the self-interest which is the driving force of the market economy. For every economic system devised for ordinary human beings must have self interest as its driving force. This does not make an economic system anti-social. The purpose

7

of such a system, indeed the very nature of an economic system, is the mechanism through which, by making what society needs most become what is most profitable to the individual, it transmutes individual self-interest into the public good. Even if the economic system were completely planned from the centre it would need a mechanism by which those who planned well, or executed their orders well, were rewarded above those who planned badly or were poor executants. No; the case against the market economy is not that it does not tend to promote the social good. The dispute is whether state control could not do better, either as an alternative, or as a supplement.

SOCIALISM AND THE STATE

In any comparison between the state and alternative social institutions which can serve the same purpose, the state starts, either with the dice loaded against it, if one is a liberal, so that it must do not just as well but much better if it is to be accepted; or with the dice loaded in its favour, if one is a fascist, so that it will be accepted unless it does much worse. Much of the current worship and denunciation of planning springs from these personal predispositions rather than from any objective consideration of particular merits.

The controversy over the role of the state is as old as human society, and so is its offshoot, the dispute about planning. We know of no society, in any place or time, in which the state has not played an active part in regulating production and distribution, or in which there have not been advocates of greater regulation and advocates of less. In our own day the advocates of greater regulation are more on the left, and the advocates of less are more on the right, but this has not always been so; the dispute about planning cuts right across left and right, and has nothing to do with the dispute about socialism.

As the pendulum swings, the powers of the state fluctuate between being too great and being too small. In 18th century England the state handicapped progress by regulating the economy excessively. The attack on the state was thus led by the progressives, and resisted by the conservatives. In the first half of the twentieth century the pendulum has been swinging the other way. The conservatives, who in the 18th century defended planning, now have to resist it; and the left, which was advocating *laisser-faire*, now has to denounce it. This is why in our day the left is associated with planning and the right with *laisser-faire*; but if we examine the basic philosophies of left and right in Britain we shall not find that either is fundamentally committed either for or against the state. Both are for and against the state according to circumstances.

Socialism, in particular, contrary to popular belief, is not committed either by its history or by its philosophy, to the glorification of the state or to the extension of its powers. On the contrary, the links of socialism are with liberalism and with anarchism, with their emphasis on individual freedom, and in opposition to the extended state. The nineteenth century socialists were not predominantly well disposed to the state, and in the blue prints of socialist society which they constructed the state receives frequently only a minor role. The state, for example, plays little part in the socialist schemes of Robert Owen, or William Morris or J. L. Bray. Marx, of course, tried to discredit all pre-Marxian socialists by dubbing them ' utopian '; but even Marx says little about the role of the state in the new socialist society, and that little is derogatory. It was Lenin, not Marx, who made ' the dictatorship of the proletariat ' the central feature of Marxian socialism. Apart from Lenin, the only other important socialist in the nineteenth century whose socialism essentially involved a powerful state machine was Sidney Webb. The Fabian Society never wholly followed Webb in his glorification of the state even in his own day; and the leader of the next generation of Fabians, G. D. H. Cole, was a fervent exponent of Guild Socialism, a form of socialism in which the state has only a very attenuated role. For Fabians the last word on this subject was said not by Sidney but by Beatrice Webb, who wrote in 1894:

How far, I wonder, will the collectivist principle carry us? The thinkers of fifty years ago believed as firmly in individualism as we believe in collectivism—probably more uncompromisingly; for the men and women of today distrust general principles even though they be prepared to use them. And yet it is easy to see now that the settled conviction of the individualists that government should be limited to keeping the ring clear for private individuals to fight in, was based on the experience of a one-sided and corrupt participation of the government in industrial organisation, and not on any necessary characteristic of state action. Face to face with the govern-ment action of their own day they were to a large extent right. Is it not possible that it is the same with collectivism? Public administra-tion is the alternative to private enterprise, and since private enter-prise is corrupt and selfish we propose to supersede it by democratic control. But it is, on the face of it, as unlikely that the collectivist principle will apply all round as that the individualist principle would solve all the social problems of fifty years ago. I do not think that we Fabians believe in more than a limited application of the collectivist principle; though, as practical politicians we think that we are as yet nowhere near the margin of cultivation, that we can cultivate this principle vigorously for all that it is worth, in all directions without exhausting its vitality. But of one thing I feel certain. The controversy which seems to us now so full of signi-ficance and import will seem barren and useless to our great-grandchildren; they will be amazed that we fought so hard to establish one metaphysical position and to destroy another. (*Our Partnership*, pp. 117-8.)

Opposite views of other socialists could equally be quoted, for there is no single socialist view of the state or of the part that it should play. The fact is that it has been with socialists, as it has been with liberals and conservatives, that some are for extending the powers of the state, and some for reducing these powers. The Liberal Party, after all, once had a Cabinet that included Asquith, Winston Churchill and Lloyd George, with as diverse a collection of views on the state as one could find anywhere; and the Conservative Party now runs in harness Winston Churchill and R. A. Butler. The dispute on the role of the state is not a dispute between parties, but runs right through the parties themselves.

Socialists have rather lost their perspective of this, and have sometimes seemed to welcome every extension of state powers. Perhaps this is because the two most recent influences, Lenin and Webb, were both worshippers of the state. But some confusion is also due to misunderstanding the socialist attitude towards property. Socialism and nationalisation of property are now commonly identified, but this is as great an error as the identification of socialism and the extended state. Socialism is not, in the first instance, about property any more than it is about the state. Socialism is about equality. A passion for equality is the one thing that links all socialists; on all others they are divided. Because they are concerned about equality socialists have to be concerned about property, since the present system of property is the most important cause of inequality. But subject to the over-riding claims of equality, socialism is not committed to any one way of dealing with property, and property can be handled in many ways that are not inconsistent with socialism. For example it can be redistributed so that each family has the same amount; this is what is done after agrarian revolutions, and though it retains individual ownership of property it is not inconsistent with socialism, as Tito has recently reminded Stalin, so long as the distribution is just, and so long as there is enough land to go round without condemning each family to work on too small and uneconomic a unit. Redistribution of land is frowned on by socialists in overcrowded Europe, but it is the essence of socialistic objectives in the newer and less crowded parts of the world. Or, secondly, property can be handed over to the workers to be operated cooperatively, on a profit sharing basis; this, and not nationalisation, was the favourite of socialist writers in the 19th century. Even in the third alternative, where property is nationalised, the role of the state is not necessarily large; the state can hand industries over to public boards and tell them to get on with the job without any central planning at all, leaving it to the public trust to buy and sell in the market, and to be regulated by demand just as would any private firm. So long as these different ways of handling property are all based on equality we cannot say that one is more socialist than the others, for socialism is not a particular way of dealing with property; it is a demand for equality and social justice.

It is also a demand for individual liberty. In the dispute about the powers of the state the traditions of socialism are rooted in liberalism. The bias of socialists, in recent times, has come to be in favour of using the state in place of other social institutions, but this is only a recent growth. The real traditions of socialism are opposed to this. The liberal tradition is to hand nothing over to the state that cannot be done nearly as well by some other social institution. Socialists who cannot go as far as this should at least pause before assuming that every suggested extension of the state has the traditions of the socialist movement on its side.

THE MARKET ECONOMY

The object of this digression has been to prepare the ground for impartial consideration of the merits of visible and invisible controls. The dispute, we have seen, is not about objectives but about efficiency. The market economy tends to control production and distribution in the public interest; the question is whether planning could not do better, either as an alternative, or as a supplement.

Even the greatest worshipper of *laisser-faire* has never suggested that there should be no state. Everyone agrees that there are certain minimum functions for which it is absolutely essential. Adam Smith listed defence, justice, education and roads and communications. Economists following in his footsteps have expanded the list, and reduced it to general principles. Enshrined in the textbooks as beyond controversy, the state has duties in respect of (*a*) things which only the state can enforce (e.g. justice, defence); (*b*) things which diffuse benefits for which the beneficiaries cannot be charged (e.g. lighthouses); and (*c*) things in which the judgment of the state is superior to that of the citizens. This last is a growing category: the state now claims to know better than its citizens for how many years they should send their children to school, between what hours they should drink, what proportion of income should be saved, whether cheap housing is better than cheap cigarettes, and so on. Whether any particular case fits into one of these categories is frequently open to dispute, but the categories are well accepted as laying the absolute minimum of functions for the state.

The case against *laisser-faire* is much more formidable than this. It rests on the following counts.

First, under a *laisser-faire* system income is not fairly distributed; and as a corollary of this, less urgent goods are produced for wealthy people while the poor lack education, health, good food, decent houses and ordinary comforts which could be supplied instead. This is no longer denied. The price mechanism rewards people according to the scarcity of the resources (labour and property) that they possess, but it does not itself contain any mechanism for equalising the distribution of scarcities. For justice in distribution we have clearly to summon the forces of the state.

The second weakness is related; the market mechanism does not humanise the wage relation. This is not a simple issue. Employment for wages arises out of the fact that the workers do not own the instruments with which they work. Some socialists have wished to abolish this relation altogether by redistributing property to the workers, as is done in agrarian revolutions, to be worked either individually or in cooperative groups. Any other solution, whether it leaves property to capitalists or hands it over to the state, retains the wage relation, and can seek only to humanise it by guaranteeing the worker's rights, and by insisting on his sharing in decisions. Of course it is arguable that in perfect competition and in full employment employers would have to court labour, so that the price mechanism, rid of its imperfections, would ensure to labour protection of its rights. Perhaps it would, but the state is a much more certain protection.

This brings us to the third defect of the market economy, its instability. Private enterprise in the creation of money produces cycles, unemployment and misery. To be sure, state enterprise in the creation of money has had no better record; the case for private enterprise in this field rested for centuries on the unchallengeable ground that control by the state had always proved to be much worse. The present unanimity of British thinkers in favour of state control of money (there is no similar unanimity in the U.S.A.) is very recent, and due only to conviction that new secrets have been discovered which reverse the advantages in favour of the state.

Equally inadequate, on the fourth count, is the market's handling of foreign monies. The case that foreign trade is self-regulating was argued long and stoutly by the protagonists of *laisser-faire*, but the same advances in monetary theory have now finally exploded this myth. Foreign trade must be regulated by the state.

Fifthly, the market economy is ineffective in coping with major change. Where resources need to be moved in considerable degree, its methods are too slow and cruel. Scarcities are not quickly eliminated, with the result that a few persons receive abnormally large incomes at the public's expense, and that scarce commodities are unjustly distributed; and at the same time over-production is not quickly reduced, with the result that other persons suffer abnormally low incomes. State action to speed the mobility of resources is clearly needed.

Next, the market economy is wasteful. Competition induces producers to improve their techniques; but it also induces them to spend heavily on sales promotion, and to evade standardisation. But here the case is not so clear. The case for *laisser-faire* in the 18th and 19th centuries was the wastefulness and stupidity of bureaucratic operations; on the subject of waste we must clearly not proceed by simple generalisations.

This part of the case against the market economy is bound up with the final count, the fact that the merits of the market depend on the existence of competition, and that perfect competition is rare. It is clear that nothing in the market mechanism itself either establishes or maintains competition. Only state action can assure competition. In this, as in so much else, the market economy cannot function adequately without positive support from the state.

PLANNING BY DIRECTION

It has been possible to state the counts in this indictment of *laisser-faire* so briefly because they are now accepted by most serious political thinkers. There are no longer any believers in *laisser-faire*, except on the lunatic fringe. There are many who denounce planning in fierce language, and who appear by implication to be arguing for *laisser-faire*, but, on closer examination there are always a few pages in their books which give the game away. The truth is that we are all planners now.

That is not to say that we believe in all forms of planning or in complete central planning. *Laisser-faire* can be complete, or it can be modified by state action at many crucial points. Similarly planning can be complete, or it can be combined with a market economy in various degrees.

In fact, the central issue in the discussion of planning is not whether there shall be planning but what form it shall take, and in particular whether the state shall operate through the price mechanism or in supercession of it. Suppose, for example, that the government decides that, in the interests of children's health, the production of milk ought to be increased. No one questions that this is a reasonable sort of decision for the government to make. But there are many ways of fulfilling this plan, some more direct than others, and some more effective. It might pass a law making it illegal for those res-ponsible for a child to give the child less than one pint of milk a day (just as it is illegal to give the child less than a stipulated amount of education). Or it might increase family allowances, and urge parents to spend the increase on extra milk. Or it might issue free milk tickets to each child, and refund the cost to milk retailers. Or it might purchase milk, and feed this to children in schools. These are measures it might take on the side of demand; they have their parallel on the side of supply. It might pay subsidies to milk producers, thus reducing the price and stimulating both consumption and production. It might set up its own state farms, and give the milk away. Or it might pass a law instructing each milk producer to increase his output by a stipulated amount. All these ways of fulfilling the milk plan are forms of planning, and of course a planner may reject some and accept others. The fundamental difference is between methods that achieve their result by persuasion and those that achieve it by command. Making milk cheaper is an inducement to extra consumption, and paying milk subsidies is an inducement to extra production; both are planning through the price mechanism. On the other hand, ordering people to purchase more milk or producers to produce more is planning by direction. The real choice we have to make is between planning by inducement, and planning by direction.

Complete planning by direction is just as much ruled out as is complete *laisser-faire*. To begin with, it cannot be applied to consumption. The Government knows better than the citizen how he should spend his income in certain spheres; we all admit this, but they are limited spheres. Bye and large the citizen demands freedom of choice in consumption; freedom to spend his money as he pleases. Rationing is abhorred, except in emergency, and so is payment of wages in kind. There must, therefore, be money, and a consumers' market. This is a severe limitation on planning, for it means that the results of planning are tested in the consumers' market. If, for example, too many resources are devoted to investment, a general shortage shows up in the consumers' market, and even if there is no general shortage, there will be particular shortages unless the balance of production is just right. Freedom of choice in consumption therefore exerts pressure for free adjustment of production to demand. The government may plan demand, by taking steps to secure a just distribution of income, but once it has done this the pressure is all against trying to plan production by direction when consumption is free.

Secondly, the worker demands freedom to choose his own job. This means that there must be a labour market, as well as a consumers' market, and that the social task of getting labour into the right jobs in the right proportions must be achieved not by direction but by inducement. This also is a big limitation on planning, for plans which can only be fulfilled by moving labour by direction are bound to fail.

There must be a market for the consumer, and there must be a market for labour. That leaves the markets for enterprise, capital and raw materials in the balance. The manager of a firm (private, cooperative or state trust) has to be able to sell what he produces, and has to attract labour by inducement. Should he be free to adjust himself in markets for enterprise, capital and raw materials, or should he produce what he is directed to produce with resources that are allocated to him?

There is nothing in the case for planning which requires the choice of methods that put industrial managers into a straight jacket. There is, we have seen, a formidable case for regulating markets in many ways, and with many objects in view, but nothing in this case calls for issuing directions to managers which diminish their freedom to adjust production to the market forces of supply and demand.

There is, on the other hand, a formidable case against planning by direction, and in favour of using the market.

In the first place, the central planner, who issues the directions, cannot hope to see and provide for all the consequences of his actions. The economic system is exceedingly complex. If you plan to increase the output of watches you must at the same time plan to increase the output of everything complementary to watches, i.e. everything used with watches or in making watches, and to reduce the output of all substitutes for watches and the constituents of substitutes. Now no single person can make a complete list of all the complements and substitutes of watches, or decide what will be all the economic effects of having more watches. And even if he could make a list for watches, he would need also to make a separate list for each of the complements and substitutes, each of which has to be planned, and again separate lists for each of their complements and substitutes, and so on. It is because of this complexity that the fulfilment of plans by direction is always so unsatisfactory. Thousands of engines are produced, but they have to be stored through shortage of ball bearings or of screws. In planning by direction the result is always a shortage of some things, and a surplus of others. Planning through the market (e.g. the state placing an order for watches, or paying a subsidy) handles all this better because, in any sphere that is affected by the decision to have more watches, the flow of money and the adjustment of prices acts as a 'governor', turning on or off automatically without any central direction.

Secondly, and for the same reason, planning by direction has to be inflexible. Once the planners have made the thousands of calculations that are necessary to fit the plan together, and have issued their directions, any demand that any of the figures be revised is bound to be resisted. The plan once made must be adhered to simply because you cannot alter any part of it without altering the whole, and altering the whole is too elaborate a job to be done frequently. The price mechanism can adjust itself from day to day, the flow of money alters, and prices and production respond; but the economy planned by direction is inflexible.

The third defect follows from these two. As the plan proceeds fulfilment is bound to be imperfect—even if the plan was perfect when it was made, conditions change. Firm X has been given a permit to buy coal; but there has been a strike, or an accident, or bad weather, and it cannot get its allocation of coal. It therefore wants to buy oil, but the oil has all been allocated, and a complete reallocation of oil is too big a job to undertake at short notice. So firm X must close, or it must buy an allocation of oil from some other firm whose need for oil is not so urgent. This has had, in most centrally planned economies, the curious consequence that the plan works smoothly only because it is supplemented by black markets in which firms can adjust themselves to changing conditions. However, given adequate stocks, a centrally planned economy

B

could carry its mistakes without interrupting production, just as in a market economy it is mainly the existence of stocks that acts as a buffer for the numerous errors made by private entrepreneurs. The main reason why centrally planned economies work always in an atmosphere of scarcity and of hit and miss is that central planners usually forget how important it is to plan for an adequate holding of stocks, but this error is not itself inherent in central planning.

To the inflexibility and errors of planning by direction we must add its tendency to be procrustean. It is hard enough to step up the output of watches if there is only one kind of watch; if there are two kinds of watch it is more than twice as hard, and it gets progressively harder the more different types of watch there are. Central planners in consequence are always tempted to excessive standardisation, not because they think that standardisation is good for the public, but because it simplifies their job. Standardisation is frequently an engine of progress; but it is also frequently the enemy of happiness, and in foreign trade it is in many lines fatal to success.

Related to this is the stifling effect of direction on enterprise, and this is a consideration of the utmost importance in a country like the United Kingdom. This is a country which lives by foreign trade. We built up this trade by being first in the field of mass production of standard commodities. But today other nations are as good as we are at this game, if not better, and we can hold our own only if we are constantly in the vanguard pioneering new ideas; inventing new goods and processes, trying them out on the market, adjusting rapidly in accordance with consumer reaction, and so on. None of this can be foreseen, and so none of this can be planned from the centre. The future of the country depends on bold and free entrepreneurship; on people with new ideas being free to back them against all opposition, to get what resources of capital, labour and raw materials they need without bureaucratic hindrance, and to test out the market for themselves. Any form of planning which prevents this permanently, or for long periods, will be the ruin of Great Britain.

And finally, the more one tries to overcome the difficulties of planning by direction, the more costly planning becomes in terms of resources. We cannot plan without knowledge, so we must have elaborate censuses, numerous forms and an array of clerks. We cannot issue thousands of licences rapidly without thousands of clerks. The better we try to plan, the more planners we need. The Soviet Census returns over 800,000 'economists', who are mostly administrative staff connected with planning. The price mechanism does the same job without this army of economists, who are thus released for useful work in the mines and the potato fields. To be sure, the market economy also has its army of hangers-on, who contribute to profit making rather than to production—its contact men, sales promoters, stockbrokers and the like, but they are not as essential to it as are the planners to planning.

On account of its complexity, planning by direction does not increase, but on the contrary diminishes democratic control. A plan cannot be made by 'the people' or by parliament or by the cabinet; it has to be made by officials, because it consists of thousands of details fitted together. Its results are embodied in thousands of administrative orders and decisions, of which parliament and ministers can have only the briefest knowledge, and which provide innumerable opportunities for corrupting the public service. The more we direct from the centre the less the control that is possible. When the government is doing only a few things we can keep an eye on it, but when it is doing everything it cannot even keep an eye on itself.

We said a moment ago that it is by little more than the swing of the pendulum that in these days it is the left that chiefly advocates more planning. It is therefore no surprise to find that the case against planning by direction and for using the market economy has been forcibly put by the arch-communist Leon Trotsky, who himself experienced the failure of excessive direction in the period of War Communism in Soviet Russia. This is what he says:

If there existed the universal mind that projected itself into the scientific fancy of Laplace; a mind that would register simultaneously all the processes of nature and of society, that could measure the dynamics of their motion, that could forecast the results of their inter-reactions, such a mind, of course, could *a priori* draw up a faultless and exhaustive economic plan, beginning with the number of hectares of wheat and down to the last button for a vest. In truth, the bureaucracy often conceives that just such a mind is at its disposal; that is why it so easily frees itself from the control of the

market and of Soviet democracy. . . . The innumerable living
participants of the economy, State as well as private, collective as
well as individual, must give notice of their needs and of their
relative strength not only through the statistical determination of
plan commissions but by the direct pressure of supply and demand.
The plan is checked, and, to a considerable measure, realised through
the market. . . . Economic accounting is unthinkable without market
relations. (*Soviet Economy in Danger*, pp. 29-30, 33; quoted in
Lerner, A.P., *The Economics of Control*, pp. 62, 64.)

PLANNING THROUGH THE MARKET

The obvious moral of all this is that our aim should be to
preserve free markets wherever possible. The manager of an
industrial establishment, whether private or public, should be
left free to adjust his concern to market conditions; to make
what he can sell, and to make it with whatever combination of
resources he can most cheaply buy. This does not mean that
he will be free from control; on the contrary, he is the servant
of the market, which controls everything that he does. Neither
does it limit the scope of planning. For the state can do all the
planning it wants by controlling in its turn the market which
controls the entrepreneur. The state can plan as much as it
wants, but it should plan not by direction but by manipulating
the market.

Thus if it wishes firms to make more of the sorts of goods
that the poor buy and less of the sorts of goods that the rich
buy, there is no need for a cumbersome machinery of allocations and controls. It can increase the taxation of the rich, and
reduce the taxation of the poor; or it can subsidise the goods
it wishes to encourage, and tax those it wishes to discourage.
If it wishes to increase the production of wheat at the expense
of other agricultural products there is no need for a multitude
of forms, clerks and agricultural committees to fix a wheat
acreage for each of 350,000 farms; it has only to raise its
guaranteed price for wheat, or to increase its wheat subsidy. If
it wishes to encourage exports at the expense of home consumption it need not give each firm an export allocation; it
can take money out of the home market by increasing taxation,
or it can alter the foreign exchange rate, or it can increase the
purchase tax on goods sold in the home market, or it can pay
subsidies on exports. And if it wishes to promote capital

formation at the expense of consumption it can, on the one hand, either subsidise investment or make investments itself, and on the other hand, it can simultaneously discourage consumption by taxation. In every case there is the choice between direction and inducement, and in every case inducement brings the same final result, without the costs of bureaucratic control.

Fundamentally, where planning parts company with *laisser-faire* is not in rejecting the market economy controlled by demand, but in arguing that demand itself is not sacred, but something that should be manipulated by the state. Once this is realised there is no need for planners to cling to cumbersome types of planning when they have at hand methods that can make planning work as smoothly as *laisser-faire* and with far superior results.

What makes it impossible to rely exclusively on planning by manipulating market demand is the immobility of resources. This kind of planning relies on inducement to bring about a supply large enough to meet market demand. Suppose, for example, that it is desired to increase the consumption of milk and that the method chosen is to distribute free milk in schools. The total demand for milk is thus increased, and its price tends to rise. If a small rise in price is sufficient to induce a large flow of resources into milk production, supply will keep pace with demand, and no further action will be required. But if it is not, there will be either a large increase in the price of milk, or a shortage for ordinary consumers, and in either of these cases further action will be demanded, either to keep the price at a reasonable level, or to allocate the limited supplies fairly, or both.

Since, therefore, the real cause of the trouble is the immobility of resources, it follows that the most important measures to be adopted are those which augment the supply. Price control and rationing may also be necessary, but since they are only necessary until such time as the supply can be augmented, they are subsidiary to measures that augment supply, and the efficiency of planning is to be judged not by the excellence of the system of rationing and price controls, but by the speed with which shortages are eliminated and price controls and rationing rendered unnecessary.

This is one of the weakest spots in contemporary planning. Governments are usually so fully occupied in enforcing measures to ensure fair distribution of commodities in short supply that they forget the prior importance of taking steps to eliminate the shortage. Their error, however, is no greater than that of the anti-planners, whose arguments always tacitly assume away the immobility of resources. In their system the market itself will equilibrate demand and supply overnight, so that interference with prices is bound to be mischievous. But the truth is that while as a general principle it is best to operate through the market, temporary shortages will always emerge, and they may demand drastic measures of two kinds—measures to spread supplies equitably, and measures to augment supplies.

PRICE CONTROL

The first distinction which has to be made is between general shortages and particular shortages. A general shortage of goods in an economy is a monetary phenomenon, due to monetary inflation, and the appropriate remedy for it is not general price controls but disinflation. As we shall see in Chapter III, inflation damages an economy in so many ways that the proper way to deal with it is not to try to treat its symptoms, with such measures as price controls, but to eliminate the root cause. In wartime disinflation is difficult because the government is not able to control its budget; but in peacetime it can control its budget, and through its budget the total flow of money, and this is much easier to do than it is effectively to operate general price controls, with rationing, and without black markets. Price control is defensible only when it is particular, and not when it is general.

A particular shortage is distinguished from general shortage by the shortage in one part of the economy being balanced by over-abundance elsewhere. The particular shortage causes prices to rise; suppliers receive an abnormal amount of money, and make abnormal profits. This extra money, if the total quantity of money is just right, must come from other parts of the economy, where suppliers must be suffering abnormal losses. Unless the shortage in some parts is balanced by over abundance in others, the shortage is not particular but general, and the remedy is not price control but disinflation.

If the shortage is particular, and the commodity is essential, then its price may have to be controlled. If the commodity is not essential, there is no need to control its price; the high price will encourage consumers to economise on it, which they can do easily because it is not essential, and which is what they ought to do. If it is an essential consumer good its price must be controlled, otherwise the poor will suffer hardship. Of course when we eliminate poverty by distributive measures ensuring a just distribution of income this argument will lose its force; but, in the meantime, essential consumer goods in short supply must be price controlled. If the commodity is an essential raw material or producer goods its price must again be controlled, lest it enter into other prices at all stages of the economy with a snowball effect. This argument, too, is easily over-done. If money is firmly in control the rise of some prices should not be able to promote a general rise in the price level, for the abnormal flow of money in one direction will be balanced by abnormal losses and downward pressure on prices elsewhere.

Effective price control depends on quality control. Price control cannot work at all unless the article or service whose price is being controlled can be described in exact specifications, otherwise suppliers effectively escape control by reducing quality. To lay down specifications is most difficult where the commodity is a service, such as restaurant service or retailing, but it is also difficult wherever the commodity varies widely in quality. Control then demands specifying a standard article (e.g. 'utility') or service (e.g. standard meal), and compelling suppliers to supply this exclusively or in the main. This is seldom wholly satisfactory, and cannot in any case be done if no suitable standards can be framed.

Finally, price control leaves demand in excess of supply, so there will be shortages, queues and black markets unless demand is cut down to the level of supply. This can be done by taxation or by rationing. Rationing may take many forms. Each person may be given a definite weekly quota, as of sugar. Or the commodity may be put 'on points' with other scarce commodities, and each person may be given a quota of points to allocate between these commodities as he chooses. Or the ration may be varied in quantity according to each individual case, as is done with petrol or raw materials, where priorities are established. Rationing is easier to administer if it is fair to give everyone an equal share than it is where priorities have to be established and each case considered separately, and in the latter event the administrative task may be most burdensome and costly. All this is avoided if the demand is reduced to the level of supply simply by placing a tax on the commodity. This is the best way to ration commodities that are not very essential, and it can also be applied to essential commodities if part of the proceeds of the tax is paid out to deserving classes who would otherwise be unfairly deprived of their share of the commodity by the imposition of the tax—this can be done easily if the classes are recognisable, by increasing allowances such as pensions, children's allowances or social insurance benefits, by appropriate adjustments of taxation, or by subsidy. The choice between administrative rationing and taxation must be made in each case on its particular merits, but there is no doubt that some form of rationing should almost always accompany price control.

So much for price control and demand. At the same time price control has also important effects on supply, which are often neglected, but which make it a dangerous instrument to use. For example, the state may wish the poor to be able to get bread at a price much below its cost of production. If it then fixes the price of bread at this low level, and does nothing else, the consequence is that the producers of bread turn to something else, and the supply of bread is reduced. Similarly, rent control is making it so unprofitable to keep working class houses in a state of repair at the high level of building costs that exists today, that many landlords are abandoning their property, and the supply of well-maintained houses available to the poor is thus contracted. Whenever a price is fixed below the market rate, the supply is thereby curtailed, and if the state does not desire the supply to be curtailed it has the obligation to accompany price control with offsetting measures restoring and increasing the inducement to supply. Price control of bread must be accompanied and offset by a subsidy to wheat. Rent control has had to be offset by subsidies to new building, and is proving harmful without subsidies toward repairs.

There is here an important distinction between controlling inducements to a whole class of persons, and controlling inducements only to some of the opportunities open to that class. If entrepreneurs as a class have their incomes halved, whatever their enterprise, the supply of entrepreneurship may diminish much or little, or may even increase; we cannot be sure. But if entrepreneurship is penalised in the bread industry but not elsewhere, or in the letting of houses but not elsewhere we can be quite certain what will happen; entrepreneurs will move from penalised into unpenalised industries and supplies in the former will contract. Thus must we distinguish between general controls and particular controls; the latter are far more dangerous than the former. Since the state is usually tempted to control essentials and to leave inessentials uncontrolled, the result of state control is frequently to reduce the supply of essentials and to expand the inessential. The way out is to make certain that any control which diminishes inducement is paralleled and offset by other action designed to maintain the inducement to supply.

Price control is thus a delicate instrument, easily misused; and when misused it frustrates the objectives of planning by diminishing instead of increasing the supplies of essential commodities, and by causing what is available to be badly distributed and therefore wasted. Price control should seldom be used alone; it should almost always be accompanied by rationing and by measures to augment supplies as speedily as possible, and because the enforcement of all this is cumbersome, price control should be used reluctantly and abandoned as soon as is feasible. Alas, price control is the most popular weapon of states, the most misused, and the one whose misuse has done most to bring planning into disrepute.

Governments who play with price control, without having the determination to do all that is needed for its successful use, get their economies into a mess. Inducements are distorted, and resources tend to flow to the inessential industries which are uncontrolled. Then we are treated to a spectacle that can only be called planning by exhortation. 'Targets' are published for essential industries, and Ministers make speeches urging capitalists and workers to move in the right directions. These speeches and targets, as extensive British experience in the last three years has proved, are almost wholly useless. One can plan by direction alone, or by inducement alone, but one cannot plan by exhortation alone, when the major result of one's actions is to make the inducements work in the opposite direction. Nearly all the planning done in this country in the last three years, with its apparatus of targets and speeches, has been of this character, and that is why all the targets have been unfulfilled, and why the very word 'target' has become a laughing stock. This is not planning, but merely pretending to plan. Planning is a serious business; what makes planning is not the targets, which merely express what we would like to see happen, but the action that is taken to achieve these targets. And the major source of error has been the use of price controls without the offsetting measures for inducement, which (with machinery for allocation and for enforcement) should always accompany price control.

MOBILITY

The most important thing to do to a shortage is to eliminate it. This is not the only thing to do. In the interim prices may have to be controlled, specifications issued, and supplies rationed. But all these are necessary only for so long as the shortage lasts, and are subsidiary to eliminating the shortage by augmenting supply. The quality and success of planning are to be measured not by the excellence of price and rationing controls, but by the speed with which shortages are eliminated, and by the effectiveness of the measures taken towards that end.

If the quantity of money is right there cannot be a general shortage of goods, and particular shortages must be balanced by the existence of surplus supplies of other goods. The existence of shortages is then a clear sign that productive resources are in the wrong places, and what we have to do is to get them correctly allocated between industries.

This is no easy job, as we shall see in Chapter VI. The best way to tackle it is by inducement; i.e. by raising the earnings in industries that are short of resources relatively to earnings in other industries. But inducement may work only over a long period, and only by means of sharp fluctuations in earnings—a sharp rise followed by a fall to normal levels, for example. Sometimes there are acceptable forms of direction which can be applied to end the shortage, e.g. by controlling raw materials, labour recruitment, or capital installations in ways that restrict less essential industries; but, especially where the maldistribution of labour is the principal problem, at other times we can rely only on the slow working of inducement, and then the shortage and the controls it makes necessary will last for some time.

It is here that planning by direction and planning by inducement meet. In a normally working economic system the state should be able to do nearly all the planning it wants by manipulating the market, and especially through the budget, which is the principal instrument of planning. Through the budget the state fixes the quantity of money in circulation, and thus determines whether there shall be inflation, deflation or the right balance. Through the budget it redistributes income, decides how much equality there shall be, and thus controls demand and supply and production. These general controls it supplements, again through the budget, by stimulating or retarding particular industries and services, either by buying itself, or by taxes and subsidies. The budget is not the only instrument available for planning, but it is the most important, the most powerful, and the most embracing. Perhaps in some other countries where the machinery for assessing and collecting taxes is very inadequate, and where corruption is rife in the Treasury, the budget is not powerful enough for planning. But in such countries the whole administrative machine is likely to be unsuitable for planning, and other weapons of planning fare no better than the budget. In Britain, however, it is not only the case that the arts of public finance are highly developed. But it is also important that while the citizen of Britain responds fairly well to fiscal demands, he hates other forms of control that involve direction, rationing or other dependence on administrative decision; and this is added reason for planning through the budget as much as possible, and relegating other forms of control to a subsidiary position.

But this kind of planning takes us as far as inducement will take us and no further. If there are big changes in demand or supply, and if resources are not mobile, it will have to be supplemented by direction. At the outbreak of a war, and at the end of a war, an economic system is not working normally. The movements required are large, and a whole network of controls is needed to cope with them. Similarly, a big change in the foreign trade position of a country calls for shifts of resources which cannot be accomplished rapidly, and which necessarily subject an economy for a long period to widespread controls. As conditions become normal it should be possible to dispense with such controls; if the opportunity has really been taken to spread resources correctly between industries the shortages should disappear. If conditions were to become stationary, all physical and price controls should disappear, and the budget remain the single instrument of planning. But of course conditions do not become stationary, and it is not desirable that they should. In normal conditions the budget will be the principal instrument of planning, but because of immobilities it will have to be supplemented by controls in all those parts of the economy where there is marked disequilibrium between demand and supply. The issue is not whether to plan or not to plan. It is simply how far planning can be done through the budget, and how much extra control we must have. This will be elaborated further in the chapters that follow.

CONCLUSION

It may be useful to summarise the conclusions of this chapter.

(1) The issue between planning and *laisser-faire* is whether we can use the visible controls of state action to improve on the invisible social controls exercised by the market.

(2) This is an issue that must be argued; there is no *a priori* case for using the state in place of other social institutions that serve the same purpose.

(3) The argument produces a formidable list of defects in the market, which state action is required to eliminate.

(4) The state can use different forms of planning to achieve the same purposes; planning by direction is much inferior to planning by inducement.

(5) In planning by inducement the state manipulates the market to secure its objectives.

(6) Manipulating demand is not enough because resources move too slowly in response to inducements. Other controls are also needed temporarily.

(7) Price control and rationing are frequently necessary in the interest of equity, but they do not solve the fundamental problem, which is to get productive resources correctly allocated.

(8) The principal objective of planning by direction should be to overcome immobilities, and the speed with which this is achieved is the true measure of the quality of planning.

(9) The main instrument of planning is the budget, but this may need to be supplemented by planning by direction wherever there is marked disequilibrium between demand and supply.

II

Fair Shares for All

THE first aim of socialists, prized above all others, is equality of income. Equality is desired for its own sake, in terms of moral justice, and it is desired also because the surplus of production should be used not to provide luxuries for a few but to abolish poverty, with its evil consequences of ill health, squalor, ignorance, ugliness and the waste of hundreds of millions of human lives. Fortunately, men have ceased, at least in this country, to dispute that it is the duty of the state to even up the distribution of income; the questions left are only how much and how.

Here there are two quite separate issues, relating to income derived from personal effort, and income derived from property.

Very few people believe that there should be complete equality of income irrespective of work done. A society that did not reward hard work more than slothfulness and skill more than incapacity would soon be reduced to dire poverty. There have been many communist experiments in the world's history, but they have never prospered, either in wealth or in numbers, and have not lasted long. The need for differentials is universally accepted; what is argued is that the current range is much too wide. No man is worth £10,000 a year, and, in our present state of poverty, with the great majority of the people earning less than £6 a week, only a few very exceptional men deserve to exceed £2,000 a year.

Income from personal effort is however a secondary issue, for it is income from property that accounts for the great inequality of incomes, both directly, because the income from property is very unequally distributed, and indirectly because part of the inequality of earnings from personal effort is due to the inequality of property incomes. If this source of inequality were abolished very few people would complain of the inequality of incomes from effort that remained. The fundamental socialist attack is thus an attack upon property, and demands either an egalitarian distribution of property or the abolition of private income from property.

All modern governments are egalitarian and seek to eliminate extremes of income. This can be done in two ways. The first is to redistribute income through taxation, and the second is so to alter the basic factors determining the distribution of income that the distribution of income before taxation becomes more equal. The method most used is the first; all modern governments effect some redistribution of income through taxation. In fact, it is arguable that some of them, especially the U.K. government, have pushed this method as far as it can go, if not indeed too far. The second method, which involves altering the distribution of property ownership and the whole class basis of society, is also used to some extent by modern governments, but only to a small extent, and it is here that the greatest changes are likely in the future.

REDISTRIBUTING INCOME

Redistribution proceeds by levying on the incomes of the rich, and using the levies to add to the incomes of the poor.

The now traditional British method is to put a floor to poverty by providing the working classes with a number of free or cheap services, notably medical service, education, social insurance, cheap housing, and, in very recent times, cheap food. The alternative, before 1939, was to pay out to the working class weekly cash benefits equivalent in amount, which they could use as they desired, e.g. by spending more on trips to the seaside if they preferred this to cheap housing. Since 1939 taxation imposed on the working classes has so greatly increased that the alternative is rather simply to reduce *pari passu* working class taxation and the service made available. The argument for the alternative is that it does away with the bother and expense of collecting working class taxation, and at the same time gives the worker greater choice and the right to take his benefits as he pleases. The only valid objection to this is the belief that the government knows better than the working classes do how they should spend their money. Thus the working classes are made to have education whether they want it or not, and medical services, and social insurance. Here, as in so much else, there is both truth and untruth, and the line is difficult to draw. If the government simultaneously abolished housing subsidies and cut working class taxation by an amount exactly equal to the subsidies the working classes would be no worse off financially; but they would then without any doubt prefer to spend the money in other ways than on housing, and would live in overcrowded and inadequately provided houses, some because they do not know the advantages of better housing, and others because they value these advantages too lightly in comparison with other ways of spending their money. That is the case, and the only case for housing subsidies, and it is put here in its crudest form because the matter is so often discussed in left-wing literature without facing reality.

Working class taxation is now so heavy, its evil effect on incentives is so considerable, and the cost of collecting taxes is so burdensome (the Inland Revenue handles nearly twenty million assessments every year) that we ought not to keep on the budget anything which strictly involves no more than collecting taxes with one hand in order to pay them out to the same people with another. If the budget is to be used for redistribution of income, the way to do this in future is not to increase the payments to the working classes, but to reduce the taxes that they pay. We can do all the redistribution that we want to do simply by adjusting the structure of taxation, and so long as the working classes are paying any taxes at all, we should never defend any government service on the ground that it is a means of redistribution. Thus, for example, the food subsidies cannot be defended on this ground, for if we were simultaneously to abolish these subsidies and to cut working class taxation by an equivalent amount the working classes would as a whole be no worse off, and we should be saving the bother of collecting and paying out, and be having the stimulating advantages of lower taxation on incentives. (The real case for some food subsidisation is bound up with the case for wage and price stabilisation with which we deal in subsequent chapters.) But, of course, when we have said all this, there remains a substantial core of social services to be financed. What socialists have wanted is to establish a society in which every child shall grow up in pleasant homes and attractive surroundings, and with good educational opportunities; in which every adult shall be provided for in sickness and adversity; and in which the pensioner can take untroubled ease. This provides a vast sphere for government activity, however it may be financed.

The provision of such services is one plank in the floor that is put to incomes. The second plank is the enforcement of minimum wages.

Controlling the general level of wages does not have much effect on the distribution of income, except for that part of the economy that depends on foreign trade. The reason for this is that there appears, in a free and closed economy, to be a pretty steady relation between wages and prices, so that if the general level of wages rises or falls, the general level of prices rises or falls *pari passu*, and the working classes are neither better off nor worse off. We do not know why this is so, but the evidence is pretty clear, over the past century, that this is what happens.

The consequence is that working class conditions can be improved by raising the general level of wages only if at the same time rigid price controls are imposed to prevent prices from rising also. This can be done, to a small extent, with general benefit to the community, in so far as pressure on profit margins stimulates entrepreneurial efficiency, or in so far as workers produce more as wages rise. But neither of these permits this kind of adjustment to be taken very far, and if wages are raised considerably prices cannot be held down without unfortunate consequences that could be avoided if the same objective were reached—as it can be—through redistributive taxation. These consequences are, first, that it is difficult and costly, in terms of administration, to administer general price controls. Secondly, that if wages are raised all round while prices are controlled there will be serious distortion. This is because wages do not enter into the prices of all commodities in the same proportion. When, therefore, wages increase in all industries in the same proportion some industries become very much more unprofitable than others and entrepreneurs are induced to move from the less profitable to the more profitable irrespective of the social value of the industries. And, thirdly, a general increase in wages relatively to prices is bound to affect employment adversely. This is partly because some firms will go bankrupt and also because it becomes more profitable to use machinery, the price of which has risen less than wages, in place of labour. More employment is provided in the engineering trades but in all other industries workers are dismissed. It is unnecessary to launch the economy upon this distortion in order to alter the distribution of income in favour of the workers. Redistribution through taxation is much easier and more sensible.

These strictures apply only to a general increase of wages, and not to the fixing of minimum wages in depressed trades. Outside the skilled trades and the professions there are great pools of labour whose supply price is very low, and much exploitation would occur but for the work that is done by trade boards and other wage fixing machinery. This is a case for raising not the general level but the level of wages in the lowest grades relatively to the level of wages in the highest grades. This also may cause some unemployment, in so far as it does not increase efficiency, but what it does mainly is to improve the bargaining power of the weakest sections of the community at the expense of the stronger and this is very much to be desired.

Next we turn from the floor that is put to low incomes to the ceiling that is put on high incomes. The most important aspect of this is the heavy taxes imposed on the highest incomes, but more recently the rich have also had their consumption controlled by rationing.

There is a certain seductive attraction in securing fair shares for all simply by rationing out commodities, thus rendering differences of money income ineffective. But this attraction is no safer than is the fascination exerted by equal money incomes. If we are all reduced to the same level by general rationing, incentives are destroyed just as rapidly as if we are all reduced to the same level of money incomes.

In addition rationing is inferior to progressive taxation for three reasons. First, it is difficult to enforce administratively without black markets, and the wider the range of commodities included in it the greater is the difficulty and the likelier the breakdown. Secondly, if rationing is confined to essential commodities, the money which is not permitted to flow towards these commodities flows towards inessential commodities whose production becomes more profitable, and the supply of essential commodities is reduced in favour of inessentials. And, thirdly, rationing interferes with the free choice not only of the rich but also of the poor, who get fuller satisfaction from their incomes if they are allowed to choose their own combination of commodities. Rationing is useful and necessary for dealing with shortages of particular essential commodities in the interval while efforts are made to augment supplies; but as a universal or permanent way of equalisation it is inferior to taxation.

The simplest way to get a greater equality of income is to put heavy taxes on the rich and light taxes or no taxes on the poor. This has been the basis of British fiscal policy for many decades and each generation has tightened the screw. How far we have gone in this direction is not generally recognised or admitted on the left. No doubt we can and should go further, but we have indeed already gone so far that many question whether the limits of this policy have not already been reached.

The problem that high taxation poses is its effect on incentives. In the days when the standard rate of income tax was sixpence in the pound this could be neglected. But when the standard rate is nine shillings in the pound and surtax on higher incomes brings marginal rates up to 19s. 6d. in the pound the effects of high taxation on incentives have to be taken into account. Actually, the major error in this field is not the amount of taxation but the structure of the income tax. A man who pays nine shillings in the pound is not in fact paying 45 per cent of his income to the Inland Revenue; allowances may be reducing the average rate that he pays to something like 20 per cent. What affects incentive, however, is not the average rate but the marginal rate, and the sensible thing to do is so to reconstruct the basis of taxation that the marginal rate is no longer in excess of the average rate. This would make the standard rate of income tax very much below what it is today—probably less than half of what it is today—and permit higher taxation to be levied in the upper ranges with smaller disincentive effects than there are at present. Several schemes have been suggested with this effect. For example allowances might be taken out of the assessment. Every person who earns an income could be entitled to draw a marriage allowance and an allowance for each child in cash from the post office in extension of the present system of family allowances; a low standard rate of say 2s. 6d. in the pound could then be levied on all income received up to say £500 a year, and beyond this point additional flat rates could be imposed. Such a reform would also greatly reduce the administrative cost and the inconvenience of the present system. If only for the sake of administrative simplification it ought to be adopted; but in addition some such reform must be adopted if further redistribution of income through taxation is to be possible without killing the goose that lays the golden egg.

EQUALITY OF OPPORTUNITY

Nevertheless whatever reforms may be made in the system of taxation, the danger to incentives remains a severe limit on the possibility of redistributing income through taxation. It is therefore all the more important to take measures to increase equality of income before taxation.

The distribution of income before taxation is determined by two principal factors, the distribution of property and the distribution of skill.

It is the shortage of skills which explains the differences in remuneration for work. Doctors earn more than miners because in relation to the demand for doctors there is a much greater shortage of doctors than there is of miners. If every child in the community could become a doctor at no cost, doctors would not be as scarce as domestic servants, and would not earn much more. In order, therefore, to even out earnings from work before taxation, what we have to do is to increase equality of opportunity. The key to this is, of course, the educational system. All socialists aim at enabling all children to have whatever education their abilities fit them for without reference to the incomes of their parents, and if this state of affairs can really be achieved, differences between the incomes of different professions will be very greatly reduced. But there are also other hindrances to equality of opportunity inherent in a class society, particularly in commerce and industry where the opportunities of securing the more highly remunerated posts tend to be reserved for a narrow circle. One of the objectives of a socialistic industrial policy must be to make it possible for all those engaged in industry at any level to have the same opportunities of reaching the top, with no other restraint than their ability and fitness for the job. Equality of opportunity is the key to greater equality of income and to the classless society.

Some part of the inequality of opportunity, and the major part of the inequality of income is due to the unequal distribution of property. Property owners, it is estimated, receive about thirty per cent of the national income in payment for the use of their property, and since about two-thirds of the property in the country is owned by only two per cent of the population this gives at once two per cent of the population some twenty per cent of the national income. There is no solution to this problem other than confiscation. The nationalisation of property is no solution because the property owners are compensated in full and after the transaction is completed they are as wealthy as before nationalisation.

This is not to say that the payment of compensation when property is nationalised is a mistake. On the contrary it is the only feasible solution without bloody revolution. After a bloody revolution it is possible for the state to confiscate all property; but revolutions dissolve the entire fabric of society and are shunned by most political thinkers not because they do not desire confiscation, and not because they do not think that it is a good thing for the heads of some of the mighty to roll in the dust (which we are told on good authority is pleasing to the Almighty), but because when the fabric of society begins to dissolve no one can predict the consequences or control the ultimate result. No revolution in history has ever achieved precisely what it set out to achieve and the results of many revolutions have been exactly the opposite of what was so intended. It is better, as Charles Lamb taught, to roast a pig over a fire than to burn down a house for the purpose.

Confiscation is achieved by levying taxes on property in a more gradual fashion than revolution implies. The most popular of these taxes are those which fall at death and which, therefore, allow the property owner to enjoy the fruits of his property so long as he is alive. Death duties are doubly popular because they affect incentive less than taxes which reduce income during life time, and also because they strike at the inheritance of wealth which is itself inconsistent with equalitarian principles. An alternative to death duties which is much canvassed but is not much applied is to impose high duties, not on the amount of property passing at death, but on the amount of property inherited. If, for example, a prohibitive tax were put on the inheritance of any amount larger than say five thousand pounds the testator could prevent much of his property from passing into the hands of the tax-gatherer by distributing it in small amounts to a large number of people instead of trying to keep it intact for a small number of people. A wide distribution of property would thus be encouraged, and a much wider distribution of income would automatically follow.

A capital levy is more painful, and also presents more technical difficulties. If it is to be administered fairly it cannot be introduced suddenly because much time has to be spent on making fair assessments. This is the chief reason why it has not yet been adopted in Great Britain; the capital levy is always advocated at the heat of some crisis as if it were a solution for some immediate difficulty, and when it is realised that the machinery for administering it would take a long time to establish, interest in the levy always flags. A recurring capital levy would discourage saving and encourage capital consumption if it were levied on classes whose capital is so small that they have a real choice between consuming it and preserving it. If it were levied only on persons owning more than say £5,000 or £10,000 of capital (the average amount of capital per family is about £5,000) it would have very little effect on incentives or on saving; and if the government agreed to receive payments in kind or in securities, and used the proceeds to pay off the national debt, its disturbing effects on property values would be small.

It is quite clear that we must make much more rapid progress with the redistribution of property in the future than we have done in the past. So long as property is so unequally distributed all social problems are made much more difficult to solve. It is not merely that there are indefensible extremes of riches and poverty, with the ever present threat of revolution promoted either from within or from without. It is also that judgment on all other issues is distorted. We are unable to think straight on nationalisation because the majority of persons think of it (wrongly) as a means towards equality, instead of considering reasonably the pros and cons of public operation of industry. Workers will not abandon restrictive practices and release their energies for production and the abolition of poverty because they fear that their efforts will merely make the rich richer. The budget is strained and taxation raised to levels dangerous to incentives. And so on. If we lived in a community in which such property as was not owned by the state (and it is not desirable for the state to own all property) was widely distributed among the people, we should attain both a standard of living and a degree of social harmony and happiness that are now beyond conception. Much of the energy which statesmen, clergymen and philosophers devote to preaching to us the virtues of social peace and brotherhood, and the dangers of envy and of industrial and political strife would be much better devoted to drafting and enforcing a law for the confiscation and redistribution of property by means of a capital levy.

CONCLUSION

This chapter may be summarised in the following statements.

(1) The case for the provision of free or cheap services by the state rests not on income distribution but on the superior insight of the government, and is limited to those services whose extended use it is particularly desired to encourage.

(2) General wage control is an ineffective means of redistribution of income unless it is accompanied by general price control, and this has undesirable effects; but the enforcement of minimum wages in particular industries is necessary for the protection of depressed groups.

(3) General rationing is difficult to administer and a cumbersome way of achieving equality.

(4) The best way to redistribute income is to impose low taxes on the poor and high taxes on the rich. Reform of the income tax system is necessary in order to pursue this policy more effectively, but in any case it has already been used so fully in the U.K. that greater emphasis must in future rest on altering the distribution of income before taxation.

(5) Inequality of income before taxation is partly due to inequality of opportunity in education and employment, which the state can help to reduce.

(6) It is also due to the unequal distribution of property which can be changed by death duties and capital levies.

III

Money

THE circulation of money determines the level of prices and of employment in a country, and fluctuations in the level of monetary circulation determine whether that country shall suffer inflation or deflation. These issues are too important to be left to the control of private enterprise; that has long been agreed, and in every modern country the government itself controls the supply of money and seeks to influence the demand. Modern progress in monetary control involves not new objectives, but simply new techniques.

INFLATION

All modern economists agree what the objective of monetary policy should be; it is to stabilise the flow of money at the level just appropriate to full employment, so that there shall be neither inflation nor deflation. Unfortunately this objective is not accepted unanimously by the politicians of the left or of the right. Many on the right would prefer a regular cycle of inflation and deflation, and many on the left hanker after continuous inflation.

The right would like a cycle of inflation and deflation because it thinks that deflation from time to time is necessary to keep the workers disciplined and to induce them to work hard. It may be true that the employing classes can continue to treat their workers as they treat them now only if the fear of unemployment can be hung over their heads at regular intervals. But to socialists this is a case not for deflation but for altering the existing relations between employer and employed. Discipline must find a new basis in the consent of worker and manager to work together for common ends; of this more will be said in Chapter VII. And as for working hard, if it is true that the worker, if relieved of the pressure of fear, would prefer to work less, or less intensively, then he should have the right to do so. His standard of living will be lower, and so will that of the country as a whole, but is it not a democratic right to decide whether extra income is worth the extra wear and tear of work ?

More dangerous is the demand of the left for continuous inflation. This, too, is rooted in the class struggle, for it is thought that if there are always more jobs than men, employers will be at the mercy of their workers. This also is true; but the left-wing politicians who accept it as a decisive case in favour of continuous inflation do so only because they are unaware of the harm which inflation does to the working classes no less than to the rest of the community.

That open inflation is harmful is seldom disputed. In open inflation prices always rise faster than wages; the workers and the middle classes suffer, while employers and property owners gain. The worst losers are the middle classes, whose salaries adjust too slowly, and whose past savings lose value, but the working classes also fail to keep up with rising prices. The left is therefore pretty firmly opposed in these days to open inflation; what attracts some of its members is suppressed inflation, in which the tide of money is allowed to flow, but is prevented from raising prices by administrative controls. Suppressed inflation is less obviously harmful than open inflation, but it too has evil consequences.

First, even if prices are controlled, inflation causes profits to rise more than wages and salaries. Inflation is a condition in which people are spending on consumer goods more than those goods have cost to produce; every extra penny of this spending, if it does not eat into stocks or upset the foreign balance, must go into profits, since this is the only residual element in income. This is why, for example, profits in Britain have increased more than wages and salaries in the last three years. The fact that this has been happening has in turn set up new pressures, demands for higher wages, and for tighter price controls; but the simplest way to check the movement, and to keep profits low, would be to check the inflation.

Secondly, suppressed inflation causes resources to be sucked away from essential industries, which are tightly controlled, to inessential industries, which are left more free, and which therefore become more profitable. Frantic efforts have then to be made to tighten up raw material allocations, but the greater the inflation the more difficult it is effectively to work such controls. Power has also to be taken to direct labour, in order to discourage it from flowing to the inessential trades. All this could be avoided by ending the inflation.

Thirdly, the inflation reduces productivity. Stocks of raw materials and work in progress are run down, and the smooth flow of production is impeded. Profits are so easy that employers become careless of costs. The competitive forces cease to work, and the stimulus to efficiency is removed.

And, fourthly, inflation brings external bankruptcy. Some of the extra money is spent on buying imports, and some is spent on attracting to the home market resources that should be working for export. The balance of payments thus becomes adverse, gold and foreign reserves are used up, and eventually unless foreign countries are willing to make loans, the external value of the currency falls.

In a mild inflation the government may strive to prevent all these consequences by using administrative controls and planning by direction. But the bigger the inflation the more difficult it is to operate such controls effectively. Administrative controls are not and cannot be an efficient substitute for controlling the level of monetary circulation. The task of such controls, on the contrary, is made all the more difficult by inflation. This is the plain lesson not only for our own experience in the last three years, but also of Soviet Russia in the nineteen thirties. Many of the most difficult and tiresome problems which that country had to face in the 'thirties were due neither to the adoption of planning nor to any national instinct for authoritarianism, but simply to having to maintain a continuous struggle with an overflowing tide of money. Inflation is as great a nuisance to those who try to plan by direction as it is to those who plan by inducement.

MONETARY STABILITY

The right policy is to have neither too much money, nor too little money, but just the right amount, and the right amount is that which is appropriate to full employment, with no tendency either to inflation or to deflation.

The old techniques for achieving this laid greater emphasis on controlling the quantity of money in existence than on controlling the demand for money. The quantity of money in existence is important, but fluctuations in trade are caused as much by fluctuations in the use of money as by fluctuations in the quantity of money, and indeed normally the latter adjusts itself to the former. The runaway inflations are caused usually by the quantity of money being increased in response to government demand, and the big deflations also see the quantity of money being reduced simply because the demand for money is reduced. Firm control of the quantity of money can prevent a runaway inflation, and a severe cut in the quantity of money is also very useful when there is too much money about (as recently in Germany or the U.S.S.R.). But controlling the quantity of money in existence cannot prevent the smaller inflations and deflations that characterise the trade cycle, because they depend as much on changes in the velocity of circulation of money as they do on changes in the quantity of money. The new technique rejects the objective of stabilising the quantity of money in existence; instead, when the demand for money is increasing, it increases the quantity of money, and when the demand is diminishing it diminishes the quantity of money, so keeping the circulation of money constant.

The instrument of this control is the budget. When the circulation of money is flagging, it can be stimulated by reducing taxation and leaving the public with more in its pocket to spend. And when the circulation is excessive it increases taxation, thus reducing the amount that the public can spend. The corollary of this is the possibility of budget deficits and surpluses. These may offset each other in the long run or they may not; this does not matter. If, for example, there were a chronic tendency for the circulation of money to fall short, there would have to be a succession of budget deficits, and provided that these were no bigger than was needed to stabilise demand, they would do no harm. A deficit is harmful only when it is greater than can be justified by the gap in the circulation of money, or when, being of the right size for this purpose, the government borrows and pays interest on it, instead of simply creating more money interest free.

At one stage in the evolution of this technique it was suggested that the government should vary not the sum collected in taxes but its expenditure, spending more when the circulation of money is flagging, and less when it is excessive. Spending more is more effective than taxing less, in the sense that a given budget deficit will add more employment if it is reached by spending more than if it is reached by taxing less. But varying taxation is easier and more desirable than varying expenditure. Public works are needed even at the height of an inflation, and unnecessary public works do not become desirable just because there is a deflation. In so far as public works can be advanced or retarded without much inconvenience it is obviously sensible to use this as an additional means of stabilising demand; but the principal emphasis must be on varying the amount of taxation.

The use of this technique depends on forecasting the amount and distribution of the national income in the immediate future to which the budget relates. If there is much less than full employment, on the one hand, or raging inflation on the other, precise calculation is not necessary or possible. The Chancellor must aim at a pretty big deficit or surplus to get the circulation of money moving rapidly in the right direction, and it is only when full employment is reached, or disinflation achieved, that precise calculation becomes important.

At full employment the forecaster estimates how much resources, in money value, will be devoted to producing consumer goods for the home market, exports, investment goods, and government services. The total of these resources is also the total of the national income, because incomes come from production, and the total cost of production is simply the total sum of incomes paid out. The other side of the forecaster's balance sheet is an estimate of how people are likely to spend these incomes. If they will spend more on buying consumer goods than will be spent in producing consumer goods the prices of these goods will tend to rise, and inflation will be set in motion; if they will spend less, deflation will be set in motion. Full employment is maintained by keeping consumers' expenditure at the right level through making up any gap by having a budget deficit, and preventing any tendency to surplus by increasing the amount taken in taxes.

There must be no pretence either that this technique can be very precise, or that it can be fully effective.

Precision is prevented in the first place by slowness in adjusting taxation. Annual budgets announcing taxes that do not come into operation for some months are not good enough for a situation where, perhaps because of events abroad, there may be swift changes in the general level of activity. This, however, can be remedied; supplementary budgets can be made, and if the income tax structure is simplified, as was suggested in the preceding chapter, swift changes can be made in the standard rate.

The other obstacle to precision is the inadequacy of the statistics available to the forecaster. This also can be remedied. It is a curious fact that there is much more statistical information available about the American economy, the home of *laisser-faire*, than there is about the British. Our statistical staff needs to be strengthened, and its power to command necessary figures needs to be increased. Fortunately we need not depend exclusively on national income estimates for guidance as to the direction in which budgetary policy should move, for there are at least two other useful thermometers.

The first of these is statistics of bankruptcy. Since business managers are not infallible there are always some using resources wastefully, and if there were no bankruptcies this waste would continue. In full employment something like 2,500 companies should go into liquidation every year. If the actual number is much above this, taxes should be reduced; if it is much below this, inflation is proceeding.

A much more precise thermometer is the statistics of unemployment. Not all unemployment is due to monetary shortage. There is also a certain amount of 'frictional' unemployment due to the changes occurring in the economy every day, whether fluctuations in demand, or new techniques of production, or changes in the availability of raw materials, or seasonal changes, or others. In consequence there are always some people out of work, moving from job to job, and it is estimated that these account for between 2 per cent and 3 per cent of the occupied population. The size of this frictional unemployment depends primarily on how well the labour market is organised, and it is our duty to diminish it as much as possible so that people displaced from any cause can find other suitable work at once. We can also diminish this figure by pursuing an inflationary policy, because if the quantity of money is large enough all employers will be short of labour, and the unemployed man need not look for the right job but can get some job immediately. But if we do this, not only do we have all the usual evils of inflation, but in the labour market also it becomes impossible to distinguish between jobs that are more important and those that are less essential. If the quantity of money is just right, when one employer discharges labour there will be another employer needing labour. It will take some time to effect the transfer, but it will be the right transfer; the worker will go not just to any job, but to the right job. But when money overflows all employers need labour, and this distinction disappears. There is no longer any means of ensuring that labour gets into the right job through inducement, and we have to resort to direction.

This is a hard and unpopular thought. Unemployment is such an evil that it is hard to reject any means that would abolish it completely. But some ways of achieving an end are better than others. The way to abolish the 3 per cent of frictional unemployment is to improve the organisation of the labour market. To abolish it by bringing down the evils of inflation and direction of labour is like cutting off an arm to save a finger.

The level of unemployment can therefore be used as a gauge for monetary policy. In the present state of the British labour market if unemployment is less than 2 per cent of the gainfully occupied population there is inflationary pressure, and if it is more than 3 per cent the monetary tap should be turned on. The more rapidly the structure of the labour market is improved, the sooner these crucial figures will be lowered, and the nearer we shall come to being able to claim that the tap should be on whenever there is any unemployment at all.

Another factor which makes it difficult to eliminate unemployment exclusively through monetary policy is dependence on external trade. If there is a slump abroad, and the demand for exports falls off, workers engaged in export industries will lose their jobs. At present many of these industries are highly localised, and there are not always enough other jobs in the locality to which the workers can be transferred. A slump abroad might thus push the unemployment figure rapidly up to 10 per cent or so, without the mere injection of money into the

system having much immediate effect. The remedy for this is
to promote the mobility of resources, both human and material,
and this is such a large subject that we reserve to it a whole
chapter (Ch. VI). In a sense this sort of employment also is
frictional, because it is due to the imperfection of the labour
market; and in this sense the estimate of 3 per cent as the upper
limit of frictional employment is too low. Foreign trade, however, is such a special problem that it is better to treat separately
the unemployment that it may cause.

THE PRICE LEVEL

Once the objective of controlling the quantity of money in
existence is abandoned, and in its stead the quantity of money
is adjusted to the needs of trade, the general price level becomes
dependent solely upon the level of wages. If trade unions raise
wages prices will rise, and the quantity of money will have to
be increased in order that this should not give rise to unemployment. When there is an absolute limit on the quantity of money,
wages and prices are limited, since if they rise too high there is
unemployment, and this pulls them down again. But the new
technique abandons the price level to the discretion of the
trade unions, and many people are convinced that the result
will be that prices will move continuously upward.

Since it is undesirable for prices to rise continually, the
corollary of this technique is that the trade unions should
agree as nearly as possible to stabilise the general level of
wages. It cannot be stabilised completely. The social interest
demands that some wages be higher than others, and since,
with changing conditions, there will always be some wages
needing to move upwards in the scale, while downward adjustments are difficult to secure, the general trend must always be
upwards. This is not new; the general trend has always been
upwards, and if in the future the upward movement were confined to what is needed to adjust particular wages relatively
to the average, the general level would seem almost stable,
when compared with what has happened in the past.

Moreover, absolute stability is not required. Since productivity is constantly increasing, prices would fall constantly if
wages were stable. Now a falling price level has the disadvantage

of raising continually the real burden of debt. If therefore wages rise as fast as productivity increases, prices will be stable, and it may even be desirable that they should rise a little faster than this, so that the debt burden may constantly be eased. If by adjusting the wages of particular workers from time to time the general level of wages were made to rise by between 3 per cent and 5 per cent per annum, we should get a price level that was just about right.

Such relative stability could not be achieved unless the cost of living ceased to be subject to cyclical fluctuation. The cost of living depends to a large extent on the cost of imports, which depends very largely on American prices. If we let import prices move freely with American prices, the cost of living will rise in the upswing, and wages will chase upwards; but in the downswing the trade unions will resist a fall in wages as the cost of living falls, and can resist successfully if we maintain full employment. So wages will always rise in the upswing without falling in the downswing, and British prices will soon be well out of line with prices abroad, and the real value of the pound will be continually depreciating. We can avoid this by stabilising import prices, either by destabilising the external value of the pound, or by subsidising imports in the upswing and taxing them in the downswing. In the past three years we have pursued the latter policy, somewhat half-heartedly; prices have been rising, but not as much as they would have risen in the absence of subsidies. The Chancellor of the Exchequer has now called on the workers to agree to wage stabilisation. But they cannot be expected to accept this for long unless he applies himself with much greater determination to stabilising the cost of living, as a *quid pro quo*. To this issue we shall return in the chapter on foreign trade.

The second condition for wage stability is that wage demands should cease to be made in a competitive spiral, with each union chasing the successes achieved by other unions. There would have to be a code of rules, to determine which wages should be above, at, or below the average, and unions would have to accept a ruling from a general body representing all the unions, which would determine which wage claims should be supported. More difficult still, the rank and file members of the unions would have to be convinced that this was desirable,

D

or the trade union movement would disintegrate through unofficial strikes, and wages and prices would rise rapidly.

Before any of this could be achieved, the workers would have to be won over to the view that raising the general level of wages is an inefficient way to try to redistribute income, and therefore that wage adjustment should be confined to setting particular wages into the right relation with the general level. This in turn will not be accepted unless the workers' attention is directed to alternative and more efficient means of procuring equality, and unless they are convinced that these means are being adequately operated.

There is little hope of these things happening in the near future. Left-wing propaganda has concentrated so long and so much on the wage struggle that it will take a long time for different views to prevail. It will not, perhaps, take as long as we think. The reception given to Sir Stafford Cripps' appeal for stabilising incomes shows that if the confidence of the working classes is won, and the issues explained, it is possible for cherished beliefs to be set aside, even if only temporarily and experimentally.

This is the biggest educational job that socialists have to do. Full employment and an uncontrolled level of wages are incompatible, and sooner or later one must give in to the other. Either the workers must understand this and agree to stabilisation, or harassed governments will be tempted either to answer further wage demands with some deflation, or to follow in the footsteps of Hitler and of Stalin in controlling wages from above. To reach agreement demands a revolution not only in left wing tactics, but also in the structure of the movement; but to fail to achieve agreement means, we can be sure, revolutions no more difficult, and very much less pleasant for the working classes.

CONCLUSION

These conclusions may be summarised as follows.

(1) The aim of monetary policy should be to have the right quantity of money in circulation, not too much and not too little. Less than full employment is an unnecessary evil; and so is inflation, whether open or suppressed by price controls.

(2) The best technique is to offset tendencies to fluctuation by adjusting the level of taxation; this may also be supplemented by timing some public works appropriately.

(3) Estimates of profits, records of bankruptcies and the unemployment percentage are the thermometers of monetary policy.

(4) The wage level should be kept relatively stable; and the structure of trade union bargaining should be adapted to this purpose.

IV

Investment

THE principal urge towards planning in modern states is the desire to achieve a much higher level of investment than is likely in an unplanned society. This is often confused with planning for stability but has nothing to do with it. In early formulations of the Keynesian doctrines it was thought to be necessary to plan investment not to keep it high, but to keep it steady, because it was believed that income and employment are a direct function of investment. This is true, or true for all practical purposes, if investment is defined to include everything except consumption, as Keynesians do define it, but not if investment is meant in the narrower and everyday sense. Income and employment can be kept steady through stimulating or restricting consumption by means of budgetary deficits and surpluses, and the maintenance of full employment does not itself demand any control over investment. The reason governments plan investment, in Russia or Eastern Europe, or in the U.K., is to get a higher level of investment than would occur if investment depended solely on the voluntary savings of the public.

Investment must be matched by savings, either voluntary domestic savings, or foreign savings, or inflationary savings, or government savings. In the past the first three have been responsible for nearly all the investment that has occurred; domestic savings have seldom been sufficient, except in the richest countries, to finance the whole of domestic investment, and even they, e.g. both the U.K. and the U.S.A., were borrowers in their early days. Nowadays foreign borrowing is unpopular, mainly through fear of foreign control; the weaker countries shun it, and it is the stronger countries that resort to financing domestic investment by foreign borrowing, as we have been doing so largely in the U.K. in the past three years. Inflation (forced savings) has tended to take the place of foreign borrowing, particularly in the U.S.S.R. in the early 'thirties, and in most of Europe today. But inflation has serious evils, as we have seen in the preceding chapter. If foreign borrowing is shunned and domestic savings are insufficient, we must fall back on a large budget surplus.

Voluntary domestic savings are always insufficient in a country which seeks to achieve rapid progress, and are all the more insufficient the more there is planned equality. Since the rich save more than the poor, countries in which the national income is very unequally distributed save much more than similar countries in which there is more equality. Accordingly, the more successful are plans for equality, the more necessary become plans for investment. The planning of investment is the corollary of the planning of equality.

The alternative is to be content with a very low rate of progress. For example, in Great Britain in 1947 gross investment was about 21 per cent of national income, but 7 per cent of national income was borrowed abroad, so domestic saving was only 14 per cent; this, also, was inflated—had there been no inflation in 1947 domestic saving might only have been 12 per cent. Now it is estimated that merely to replace existing capital as it wears out requires about 10 per cent of national income. So, in the absence of inflation and foreign borrowing, net new investment in 1947 would probably not have been more than about 2 per cent of gross national income.

If net investment were kept at this level, the British standard of living would increase only very slowly, and the prospect of being able to abolish poverty and to give to everyone a reasonable standard of material enjoyment would recede into the distance. Other countries would soon surpass this country, for in other countries investment is proceeding apace. Already we are far behind the U.S.A., and for seventy years our rate of material progress has been behind that of several countries, in Europe and elsewhere. This is partly because many British investors in that time were more interested in sending their money abroad than in investing at home, so that domestic industries fell behind, and partly because, in the period between the two wars, there was so much unemployment and excess capacity in staple British industries that their owners had neither the money nor the will to re-invest. In consequence many British industries need largely to be re-equipped with modern equipment if the workers are to produce all that is possible.

The argument must not, however, be pushed too far. The claims of consumption are as real as those of investment. The purpose of present investment is future consumption, and we would be foolish to starve ourselves in the present simply to increase consumption at some later date. The Russian government, for example, imposed an immense strain on its people in the 1930's when it decided to go all for producing machinery and guns instead of butter and shoes and houses, and we should certainly not try to imitate them. In a democratic country efforts to cut consumption or to keep it low, in favour of investment, are sure to be resisted. A government may get away with planning for as much as 15-20 per cent of the national income to be used for gross investment, but if it tries to go further than this it will meet considerable resistance.

If a government wishes to carry through a large investment programme without cutting consumption, the only remedy is foreign borrowing. That is what we have been doing in this country for the past three years. For example, in 1947 national production and national consumption were just about equal to production and consumption in 1938—a little more or less. Why then did we have a large adverse balance of payments in 1947 whereas we were almost in balance in 1938? The answer is because gross investment was very much larger; in fact the increase in gross investment was just about equal to the adverse balance of payments. This is not generally realised. There are those who speak as if the adverse balance is due to riotous living by the British people; and others who allege that the standard of living is being maintained only by American charity. The truth is simply that we have been borrowing abroad to finance capital formation at home. This is a very sensible thing to do, provided that the capital is not being wasted, and that the terms on which it is borrowed are not onerous. But it is possible only so long as, and to the extent that, other countries are willing to lend. If reasonable creditors abroad cannot be found, a country cannot invest at home, beyond the point where it has exhausted its reserves of gold and foreign exchange, without cutting consumption. And since the public is certain to resist a cut in consumption, the government must limit its investment plans.

Whatever the figure at which it aims, the first principle of investment planning is that the government must have a budget surplus large enough to fill the gap between the investment that is planned and the voluntary savings that are available (including long-term borrowing from abroad). If it has not, then there will be either inflation at home, or an involuntary adverse balance of payments.

The second principle is that stocks of raw materials, work-in-progress and finished commodities are as important a part of investment as is fixed capital. For it is the existence of stocks that enables an economy to work smoothly. As soon as stocks are low productivity falls, because producers then depend absolutely on receiving a steady flow of supplies, and are held up cumulatively by chance interruptions in delivery. Normally these considerations are not important, and net investment in stocks is not required. But at the end of a war, or of an inflation, the economy is short of stocks, and a large investment in stocks is the first thing that is needed in order to get productivity as high as possible. When we remember that stocks should normally stand at between 3 and 6 months of requirements, the magnitude of the sums involved will be seen. Failure to build up stocks has been one of the principal errors of the British investment programme.

The third principle in investment planning is that investment must not be planned beyond the limits of the physical resources available, no less than the financial resources. It is no use planning for 20 per cent if the steel and timber available are enough only for 12 per cent. By all means expand the capital goods industries as rapidly as possible, so that it may become possible soon to plan for the desired level of investment. But the starting point now must be not what is desired, or what will be possible next year or the year after, but what the existing resources in the capital goods industries now permit, after making allowance for such part of their product as has to be exported. It is a common error of governments, including our own, to advance so many investment projects simultaneously that the available resources of steel, machinery, cement, labour, and so on are insufficient to cope with them all. Then there is intolerable confusion. Many projects are started, and then held up at crucial points, and instead of having a substantial number of finished projects, we get instead a much larger number of unfinished projects, most of which cannot proceed because the resources they need for finishing are locked up in other unfinished projects. It is foolish to plan for more investment than the available physical resources will permit.

In our case we have added to our problems by doing what we can to encourage investment at a time when what was needed was discouragement. We came out of the war with such arrears of investment that if all the things people wanted to do were added together they would probably amount to 40 per cent to 50 per cent of the national income for some years. There were houses to be built, private industry to be re-equipped and extended, and a vast programme of governmental projects from schools and hospitals to coal and colonial development. At other times, and in other places, the problem is the reverse of this, namely, how to stimulate investment, and the government has then to mobilise its weapons, its subsidies, low interest rates, generous depreciation allowances, and the like. But in contemporary Britain what we need is to discourage investment; that is to say to find means of checking and eliminating the less urgent projects, so that the nation will not embark on more than the 20 per cent that is the financial limit, or the still smaller figure that the physical resources can support.

How is this to be done? There is the familiar choice between direction and inducement. The government can decide to license investment, so that every single project has to be examined by its officers (at one time we took this to the limit, in the building industry, of requiring a licence for decorations costing £10), or it can make new investment so costly that all except the most urgent projects, adding up to 20 per cent, are voluntarily postponed.

The method of licensing is so cumbersome that it cannot be efficient. Who is to decide between the relative urgencies of a new bridge in Basutoland, a new hospital in Aberystwyth, a new mousetrap factory in Glasgow, or a new cinema in Oxford? The answer is that nobody can decide, and that therefore conscientious officials, fully knowing that they have not the facts on which to base a judgment, will pass everything that seems on the face of it to be reasonable. The result is always that more licences are granted than the available resources can fulfil, and that there is an unholy scramble in the course of which many of the most urgent projects are held up because the promoters of the less urgent have been more skilled in the arts of acquiring scarce materials.

To say this is not to imply that the alternative, which is to make new investment very costly, gives perfect results. It knocks out all the projects that cannot afford a high price, and some of these are urgent. But it is simpler for the government to correct this error by subsidising the projects which it considers specially urgent, so that they are able to afford the high cost of investment, than it is to launch upon the meaningless and ineffective method of licensing. Neither need the method of inducement and subsidy be costly to the government, as we shall see in a moment.

The traditional way of making investment more costly is to raise the rate of interest. It is an effective way, if the rate is raised high enough. For example, if £1,000 is invested for twenty years at 10 per cent, it must yield £117 a year for interest and repayment of capital. This would also be the annual charge if the rate of interest were kept at 3 per cent, but a tax imposed bringing the cost of investment up to £1,748. That is to say, on a twenty year investment the difference between a rate of 3 per cent and a rate of 10 per cent is equivalent to as much as a tax on investment of 75 per cent.

Raising the rate of interest may also help to increase voluntary saving, but this is much less certain. A savings campaign is very necessary in these circumstances, but raising the rate of interest does not make much contribution to this.

The objection to raising the rate of interest is that it increases the unearned incomes of lenders, doing this both at the expense of private borrowers and at the expense of the government, which is frequently in the market either for new loans or for purposes of conversion. This is not an insuperable objection, because it is always possible to adjust the taxes on unearned incomes in compensation. It seems a difficult political issue only because the left does not realise that when interest rates rise capital values fall *pari passu*, and the loss inflicted upon capitalists by this is much greater than any gain that accrues from higher interest rates. Indeed, the real objection to playing about with interest rates is precisely the fact that this causes wide fluctuations in capital values which give an unfair bonus to property owners when rates fall, and impose an unfair tax upon them when rates rise (including some of those who have responded to savings campaigns).

The alternative way to make investment more costly is to impose a tax upon it. This is not as effective an alternative in one sense. A rise in the rate of interest hits investments for long periods harder than it hits short investments. It therefore encourages people, when capital is short, to use it for purposes that yield results in the immediate future rather than for those that take time to bear fruit. And this is one of the savings that we wish to make. A tax on investment, on the other hand, hits all investments equally, irrespective of their duration, and is therefore inferior to raising the rate of interest in the sense that it does not discriminate sufficiently against investments of long duration.

This argument is perhaps less forceful now that the majority of investments of long duration are in projects directly under government control, such as houses, communications, and fuel, for the government is less sensitive to changes in cost than is the private investor, and not therefore so easily controlled by such weapons as the rate of interest. Some would argue the other way; that since the government tends to be extravagant in its investment projects, it is all the more important to submit such projects to the test of the rate of interest. There cannot be much in this either way. The Treasury has to learn to put a global limit on government controlled investment, so that private industry shall not be starved of capital, and it has to develop its own technique (including possibly charging a high rate of interest to Government undertakings, actually or notionally) for rationing out what is available between the various government claimants. If Parliament, public opinion, and common sense will not force the Treasury to learn this lesson, then it is unlikely to let itself be forced by permitting high interest rates to be levied upon it.

We come here to a very serious problem for which no solution has yet been found. All planning governments tend to be at one or the other of two extremes. In the one case they produce vast plans for houses, schools, hospitals, civic buildings, roads, and other forms of public works, and use up so much capital for these purposes that very little is left for productive industry, which is thus starved of capital. In the other case they fix their eyes on industrial projects, while housing gets worse and worse as people crowd in increasing numbers into towns that are building nothing but factories. Democratic governments, like that of the U.K., are particularly prone to the first error, because they win elections on programmes demanding a vast expansion of social services, while asking for the re-equipment of private industry gains no votes. Dictatorial governments, like that of Russia, and governments of backward countries anxious to industrialise are prone to the other error, and neglect to provide capital for social amenities. There is indeed no simple formula that tells us how to weigh up the respective capital needs of production and of social amenities; certainly the rate of interest (which would be the *laisser-faire* answer) cannot discriminate between the social usefulness of schools, health centres, roads, houses, irrigation works, and factories. We are here in one of those spheres of public administration where no precise line can be drawn, and where we depend simply on democratic judgment to ensure that neither extreme is adopted, to the exclusion either of productive investment or of social amenities. There are two things we can do. The first is to insist that productive enterprises should all have to pass the same tests, in their demands for capital, whether they are nationalised or in private hands; that is to say, that it is wrong that nationalised industries should be able to get capital more easily or more cheaply than private industries just because they are nationalised, and without other reference to their relative urgency and productivity, e.g. as compared with industries producing for export, or with agriculture, or with engineering. And secondly we can insist on publication and free public discussion of the annual capital budget, which shows how the available capital is to be allocated between the various claimants; of this we shall say more in the final chapter.

This digression on the control of governmental demands on capital interrupted a discussion of the relative merits of taxing investment and of raising the rate of interest as means of reducing demand to the level of supply. The first disadvantage of the taxing method, we saw, was that it does not discriminate in favour of short term investments and against long term investments, as does raising the rate of interest. The second disadvantage is the administrative problems that it raises. The simplest way to impose the tax would be to put (import or excise) duties upon those materials that are needed in nearly all investments, namely steel, timber, bricks and cement. Such a tax would be easy to collect, and though it might cause some shift to substitute materials, this would be negligible. More serious would be the fact that it would necessitate paying a drawback on exports using these materials. Exporters would find this a nuisance, and full of anomalies, but since they would be receiving money for once, instead of paying it out, they would probably bear the burden cheerfully.

Against these disadvantages must be set an important advantage. If the rate of interest is raised, investment is as it were taxed for the benefit of private lenders; but if the government imposes a tax, the proceeds go not to private lenders but into the public coffers. This has the additional advantage of providing a fund that can be used to subsidise those desirable investments which cannot afford to pay the higher cost.

To sum up, neither raising the rate of interest nor taxing investment is without disadvantage, and probably what is needed is some combination of both. Either of these is superior to setting officials to assess the merits of each project, but even this is better than to make no effort at all to keep investment projects within the limits of the available resources.

CONCLUSION

The conclusions of this chapter are as follows:

(1) The state is justified in stimulating investment if investment would otherwise be too low; but the problem of contemporary Britain is rather to check investment.

(2) There must be a budget surplus equal to the difference between voluntary savings and investment, or there will be either inflation or an adverse balance of payments.

(3) There must be adequate provision for stocks.

(4) The sum of investment projects must not exceed the physical resources available in the capital goods industries, after allowing for exports.

(5) The licensing of investment is an inefficient way of keeping this sum within the necessary limits.

(6) The best way to achieve this purpose is a combination of a high rate of interest and a tax on some of the materials used for investment.

V

Foreign Trade

IN the *laisser-faire* philosophy at its most extreme there is no place for a special chapter on foreign trade. No significant difference between domestic and foreign trade is recognised. Trade between London and Paris or New York does not differ from trade between Cardiff and Glasgow, and needs no special treatment. Foreign trade is self-regulating, and raises no problems that domestic trade does not raise. There may be people who still believe all this, but they are now very rare.

PROTECTION

The first breach in this position is made when it is accepted that, whatever may be the case for or against a general regulation of trade, affecting all imports and exports, there may be a case for deciding that certain particular industries should be maintained at home, to the exclusion or curtailment of imports. Two important classes are generally admitted.

First there are defence industries. In the past much of the case for protecting agriculture has rested on this ground. More recently it has become plain that the countries that win wars are not those that are self-sufficient in food, or that have a sturdy peasantry, but rather those that are highly industrialised, and the emphasis is changing now to steel, and chemicals and some branches of engineering.

The second exception recognises the fact that an industry is not at its strongest until it has attained a certain size and experience. Hence, if protection were ruled out, often the country that started an industry would be able, by competing abroad, to prevent other countries from following in its footsteps, and might succeed in making substantial profits at their expense, although, if once their industries were able to get past their teething troubles, they would be quite as efficient as that of the country first in the field. This infant industry argument is now seen to have very wide implications. For what is true of one industry is even more true of industrialisation as a whole. Countries predominantly agricultural are at a disadvantage when they start to industrialise, in competition with the older industrial countries. But, given a stage of protection, they may in due course be perfectly capable of holding their own.

Both these cases have their parallel on the side of exports. The defence argument is used frequently to justify banning certain exports, or exports of certain goods to certain countries, e.g. from the U.S.A. to the U.S.S.R. And there are many examples in history of countries trying to keep at home certain inventions or types of machinery, in order to prevent competitors from catching up.

Another restriction now widely accepted, is control over the export of capital. This is a necessary corollary of planning for equality, since, in the absence of such control, capitalists can evade equalitarian measures by exporting their capital. To prevent any capital whatsoever from being exported would be a formidable task, but the larger movements can be controlled without excessive restrictions.

BALANCING PAYMENTS

These arguments for particular prohibitions can be accepted without damaging the general case. If foreign trade is to be left to regulate itself (apart from these exceptions to which no further reference will be made), then imports and exports must balance, when invisible items and long term capital movements are included. For, if imports and exports do not balance, then the net result of foreign trade will be either inflationary, if exports are in surplus, or deflationary if imports exceed exports. The essence of the *laisser-faire* case is that this balance is secured automatically. If this is so, it follows that attempts to regulate trade are mischievous. Each person should buy in the cheapest market, whether at home or abroad; if this causes imports to rise, exports will rise also. Domestic employment cannot be increased by reducing imports, because this will reduce exports to the same extent. And the national income cannot be increased by shutting out imports, because this will merely cause resources to be diverted to produce for home consumption away from the more profitable export markets that they were previously serving. If it were true that a mechanism existed which automatically linked imports and exports, these conclusions would be beyond challenge. Foreign trade could be left to look after itself, and the state need not plan it.

The extreme *laisser-faire* position sees such a mechanism in the foreign exchange market, with freely fluctuating rates of exchange. Here exports and imports (including invisible items) are kept equal by the currency being driven to whatever level is needed to keep them equal. This follows because importers are selling the currency to get foreign currencies to pay for what they have bought, and exporters are selling foreign currencies and buying their own. Since the price will move to whatever level equates demand and supply, it will automatically equate imports and exports. But since demand and supply change, not only from day to day but even from hour to hour, the result of this free market is a rate that fluctuates constantly. It is generally agreed that these fluctuations are undesirable, and that it is more convenient and better for trade to stabilise rates of exchange.

To fix the rate of exchange, however, is to make a sharp break with *laisser-faire*, for the state is at once dragged into the picture. The rate can be stabilised only if someone agrees always to buy and sell at the stipulated rate, and that someone has to be the government or its agent.

Once the rate is fixed, some other mechanism must be found to keep imports and exports in equilibrium. The modified *laisser-faire* position is still that the adjustment can be procured automatically. If imports are too large, money leaves the country. Prices therefore fall in the country with an import surplus, and rise in those countries that have a corresponding export surplus. The fall of prices makes home produced goods cheaper than imports, and so reduces imports; it also cheapens exports, and so increases them. So long as imports exceed exports, on this view, prices will continue to fall through money leaving the country to pay for the import surplus, and so imports will be checked and exports increased until they once more balance. Similarly if exports are too large, money comes into the country, prices rise, imports become relatively cheaper and larger, exports become relatively dearer and smaller, and so the export surplus is whittled away. This process is supposed to be automatic, but in order to make sure that it should work, governments are enjoined to reinforce it. When money is coming in, they should multiply it, so that prices at home do not fail to rise; and when it is flowing out they should give an extra turn to the tap reducing the circulation of money so that prices should not succeed in resisting the fall. Thus instead of the domestic price level being independent, and the foreign exchange rate fluctuating in order to effect adjustments, the foreign rate is stabilised, and the domestic price level is required to adjust to the changing conditions of foreign trade.

The trouble, of course, is that the domestic price level refuses to behave as this theory demands. When there is an import surplus prices fall a little, but not much. The adjustment that should be effected through prices is then effected through employment. The deficiency of effective demand due to the import surplus causes employment and the national income to contract by a multiple of the surplus. Exports increase very little, because prices are not falling, and the bulk of the adjustment is borne by the domestic income contracting so much that imports are eventually reduced to equality with exports. The real alternative to a changing exchange rate is not a changing domestic price level, but a changing level of employment and of national income.

Moreover, it is not only the domestic national income that contracts by the multiple of a deficit; it is also the volume of international trade. If one country has a large export surplus, paralleled by an import surplus in the other countries, this surplus could be eliminated if each of the deficit countries deliberately cut its imports from the surplus country, and there would be no multiplier effects. But if such deliberate and discriminatory planning is forbidden, each deficit country will reduce its imports all round as income contracts, and the deficit countries will reduce their trade with each other, as well as with the surplus country, thus effecting a much greater contraction of total trade than is necessary.

The moral of this is that it is indeed true that foreign trade is self-regulating, and will look after itself without interference;

but it is also true that the results of this self-regulation may be disastrous.

If the rate of exchange is to be kept stable, governments must have the right to control imports directly, so as to keep them in line with exports without having to suffer the deflations and inflations that automatic regulation would involve. They must also have the right to discriminate against surplus countries. The choice is between a free exchange rate and planned foreign trade.

It must, however, be noted at once that this planning must follow internationally agreed rules, or we shall all be worse off than if there were no planning. Thus a government is justified in controlling imports if it has an adverse balance; but if countries with an export surplus proceed to cut imports the best efforts of deficit countries to achieve balance will be frustrated. Similarly, a deficit country is entitled to try to redress its position by depreciating its exchange rate, but it cannot succeed in doing this if the surplus countries insist on depreciating *pari passu*. International trade and exchange policy must be governed by rules, as much in the interest of the weak as in the interest of the strong. That is why the U.K., temporarily a weak country, has been right in sponsoring the Bretton Woods monetary agreement, and the International Trade Charter. Neither of these documents is perfect; but they do embody rules designed to restrict the arbitrary actions of the strong. Given that there are international rules to preserve order, the choice can be exercised between varying exchange rates and applying more direct controls.

Using the rate of exchange to equilibrate export and imports does not necessarily involve day to day fluctuations. The rate can be set at the level which is expected to be adequate over the average of a period ahead, while allowing day to day fluctuations in demand and supply to be met from day to day changes in the working stock of gold and foreign exchange reserves. This was the purpose of the Exchange Equalisation system operated during the 'thirties; the rate could be altered to meet a fundamental disequilibrium, but was stabilised in face of short term changes that would cancel out.

This technique is most appropriate to a small country whose imports and exports are competitive. In such a case the prices that the country receives for its exports or pays for its imports are outside its control, and its terms of trade are not affected by changes in the foreign exchange rate. If its currency depreciates, the prices of its imports and its exports rise correspondingly in terms of local currency, while remaining unchanged in terms of foreign currency. Production for export is thus made more profitable, and attracts additional resources; and since the world market is large relatively to the country's exports, additional exports can easily be sold. At the same time the rise in the price of imports checks demand. Exchange depreciation thus automatically reduces imports and increases exports, and will secure equilibrium if pushed far enough.

Even in this most favourable case, however, there may be snags. If the imports are essential commodities, even a large increase in price may have little effect on demand; then the whole burden of adjustment falls on exports, and the ease with which it is borne depends on how easily the flow of resources to exports responds to additional prices for exports. If this flow also is slow, the rate of exchange may be forced down very low indeed. Moreover, as import prices rise, the cost of living rises, and workers demand and receive higher wages. This can frustrate the whole purpose of exchange depreciation, which works by reducing the domestic price level relatively to world prices. If every time the rate of exchange falls, wages and the domestic price level rise correspondingly, exchange depreciation cannot equilibrate imports and exports. Even a small country, therefore, may find itself, when the exchange rate falls, trying to stabilise the internal price level by subsidising imports; and since this puts the whole burden of adjustment upon exports, it may have to take vigorous measures to increase exports directly. And it may end, if resources are slow to move, by limiting imports by licence, and stimulating exports by direction.

The larger the country the greater the snags. Exchange depreciation by a large country almost inevitably causes the terms of trade to deteriorate. Prices of imports fall somewhat in terms of foreign currency if it is a large consumer, but prices of exports also fall, and if it is a manufacturing country whose exporters base quotations on domestic costs, export prices in foreign currency may fall by the whole amount of the depreciation. Export prices then fail to rise in domestic currency, and resources are not attracted to exports. At the same time the fall of prices in foreign currency stimulates foreign demand, but unless this stimulus is substantial (i.e. unless the elasticity of foreign demand exceeds unity) the country will actually get less foreign exchange for more exports. In the long run foreign demand is elastic; buyers will change over to the sellers with lowest prices, but in the short run foreign demand is much less elastic, and exchange depreciation may worsen the position of a deficit country. The experience of the United Kingdom in the last three years is a grim example of this. We have had an adverse balance, but foreign demand has been very inelastic, and if we had depreciated the pound we would have lost heavily. On the contrary, we would have done better if we had put the pound higher. This, for example, has been the secret of Belgian prosperity. In the year June 1946 to June 1947, according to calculations made by the Economic Commission for Europe, the Belgian index of commodities available for home use (basis 1938) stood at 123, while the U.K. index was only at 95. But this was not because Belgium had recovered faster than Britain, for Belgian production was only at 94 while British production was at 108. The difference was due to the fact that Belgium was importing more than pre-war and exporting less (imports 120, exports 71 in the first nine months of 1947) while Britain was importing less and exporting more (77, 106). How did Belgium manage to finance a higher level of imports from a lower level of exports? Partly from windfall payments on invisible account. But very largely, also, by selling at high prices. In terms of dollars the Belgian export price index was at 261, while the British was at 182. 71 per cent quantum sold at 261 per cent price yields 185 per cent revenue, which is nearly as much as 106 per cent quantum sold at 182 per cent price, yielding 193 per cent revenue. The Belgians earned as much in foreign exchange while keeping their goods at home to add to home consumption instead of exporting them. British visitors to Belgium thought that the obvious signs of prosperity there were due to a greater recovery, and wondered whether this was not due to greater *laisser-faire*; but it was, in fact, due mainly to better planning of the foreign exchange rate. It is now clear that we would have gained by putting the pound higher in 1945; if its dollar rate had been 25 per cent higher we should have saved some

£600 million pounds or so of gold and foreign exchange. No doubt we could not hold the pound for ever at that level, because as industry elsewhere expands demand will become more elastic; over-valuation in the nineteen twenties, for example, proved very costly. But all this only reinforces the point that equilibrium cannot always be attained by following simple rules of exchange manipulation.

The major snag is the slowness with which resources move. If adjustment were perfect, the rate of exchange would always achieve equilibrium. As it fell, and prices of imports rose in domestic currency, domestic production of substitutes would expand rapidly, and imports would fall substantially. As export prices rose, if the terms of trade were unaffected, or as foreign demand increased and raised export prices, resources would move rapidly into export industries. Thus, whether by checking imports or by expanding exports or both, exchange depreciation would do the trick, and do it rapidly. Unfortunately the movement of resources is very slow. Once we have reached an equilibrium position we can hope to keep it without foreign trade controls if there are no major changes in demand or supply. But when we are as far from equilibrium as most countries of Europe are today, the licensing of imports and the direction of exports are essential.

A shortage of foreign currency is of all shortages the most ruinous to the attempt to plan solely by inducement, not only because it is itself difficult to eliminate without more rigid controls, but also because controls applied to imports and exports work their way through to bind almost the whole economy. It is therefore all the more desirable to eliminate this shortage as rapidly as possible, and even with the most vigorous forms of control. (That is to say, it is desirable to eliminate an import surplus if it is an unwanted surplus, which will be the case to the extent to which it is not covered by long term borrowing from abroad; a surplus financed by long term borrowing does not give rise to a shortage of foreign exchange.)

The most common cause of an import surplus in Europe today is the fact that most countries are investing more than their peoples are willing to save. The difference is paid by foreigners (in so far as it does not come out of foreign exchange and gold reserves), and takes the form either of excessive imports or of too low a level of exports. It can be eliminated by importing less or exporting more, and both of these can be enforced by physical controls, but in that case the money that would otherwise have been spent either on imports or on domestic goods now exported will most of it chase after the reduced supply of goods at home and increase the inflationary pressures. The first step towards equilibrium is therefore to mop up this money; that is to say, to increase domestic savings or to increase taxation, or if neither of these can be done, to cut investment. Monetary control can go most of the way to closing the foreign gap, and it is this that most European countries need most, even more than exchange control. But monetary control may not go all the way to eliminate the shortage of foreign currency. For even when there is no inflation, indeed even if there is considerable unemployment, it may nevertheless be the case that domestic production of the types of exports that foreign buyers like is small, and that relatively to what can be exported imports are too high. Control of imports is then necessary, and also measures to increase exports, such as the fixing of compulsory export quotas, and drastic measures to man up export industries. A country like the U.K., which has at the same time a high propensity to import, a severe maldistribution of labour, and a high degree of immobility of resources is bound to be rigidly controlled for some time. The need for these controls depends not only on the removal of inflation but also on the speed with which productive resources can be reallocated. It is immobility which principally makes physical controls necessary, and we shall revert to this subject in the next chapter.

THE TRADE CYCLE

Unfortunately, the difficulties do not end here. If foreign demand were relatively stable, changing, but only slowly, licensing and direction could be used to correct a fundamental maladjustment, and then abandoned; equilibrium thereafter being maintained solely by occasional adjustments of the rate of exchange. But foreign trade shows no such stability. It fluctuates violently both in price and in quantity, in response to the trade cycle. For many years this cycle has been dominated by the U.S.A., and it is safe to say that the fluctuations of world trade depend largely on domestic events in the U.S.A.

The first reaction to this unpleasant situation is naturally to try to reduce dependence on the U.S.A. Thus in these days schemes for starting trading clubs excluding the U.S.A. have become very popular, especially imperial preference, customs unions, and bulk trading contracts between governments. Each of these has serious technical limitations which make it much less effective than is supposed, but each has some advantages. It is very desirable that production should be increased substantially outside the United States, even apart from any question of trade fluctuations, so that the export surplus of the U.S.A. may be eliminated; and so long as that surplus persists, discrimination against the U.S.A. is also a desirable alternative to a general deflation of international trade. This case for discrimination is reinforced by the instability of American trade; until such time as the U.S.A. effectively pursues a full employment policy, nations that are planning for stable employment are justified in seeking to reduce their relations with the U.S.A.

But all this is not likely to get very far. In the first place, the United States is the world's biggest importer of raw materials, and one of the biggest importers of food. All primary producers are interested in and dependent upon this valuable market, and they transmit this dependence to the manufacturing countries who sell to them, and who would thus be affected by American fluctuations even if they themselves had no direct trade with the U.S.A. And, secondly, most countries in the world look to the U.S.A. for loans. Countries dependent on the U.S.A. either for trade or for loans cannot practise more discrimination against the U.S.A. than that country is willing to allow. The U.S.A. has already indicated how much discrimination against itself it will tolerate; this is stated in the Bretton Woods agreement, in the International Trade Charter, and in the Marshall agreements. We must use it such as it is, and we may ask for more; but to try to get more adopted in defiance of the U.S.A. is a waste of time. The other countries concerned are in no position to defy the United States. What we are most entitled to demand is that the rules of Bretton Woods be altered in two ways; first, to make it easier to declare a currency to be ' scarce ' when it is in fact scarce, and secondly, to add the power to require a country which has a persistent export surplus to appreciate the value of its currency. The latter is the easiest form of discrimination to work, and the most likely to be accepted.

We must resign ourselves to cyclical fluctuations in international trade until such time as the U.S.A. is converted to planning for stability. This means that the prices of imports, measured in dollars, will rise and fall at regular intervals, and that the domestic price level will fluctuate similarly unless special steps are taken to stabilise it.

If the foreign exchange rate is kept stable through the upswing of the cycle the cost of living will rise, and wages and the domestic price level will also be dragged upwards. Then, when the slump comes, import prices will fall. If it is then decided to keep wages stable and not to reduce them as the cost of living falls, then export prices will be high in relation to foreign prices which have fallen, and unemployment in the export trades will be severe. This might be avoided by depreciating the foreign exchange rate when the downswing begins. But this will mean that the domestic price level rises each time there is a boom abroad, but never falls; and the foreign exchange rate falls each time there is a slump, and never rises. There will thus be a cumulative inflation of domestic prices, and a cumulative depreciation of the pound. This is most undesirable. If wages and the domestic price level are to rise when foreign prices rises, then they must also fall when foreign prices fall.

Domestic prices could be stabilised by subsidising imports in the boom and taxing them in the slump, since this would keep the cost of living steady. But what then happens to exports? It is desirable that British export prices should rise when foreign prices rise and fall when foreign prices fall. Otherwise we are deliberately turning the terms of trade against ourselves in the boom, when we sell the largest quantities with the least effective competition, and the fact that they will turn in our favour in the slump, when we sell smaller quantities in acute competition, is no compensation for this. This is the policy we have been pursuing in the past three years—subsidising imports to keep wages and prices steady, and thus keeping down the prices of exports, and deliberately turning the terms of trade against ourselves. This is a foolish policy, which has already cost us several hundred million pounds of foreign reserves. If we stabilise the rate of exchange, and stabilise wages and the cost of living by subsidy, then we must raise export prices by imposing export taxes. Import subsidies and export taxes together can stabilise the domestic price level without causing adverse terms of trade, but one without the other is too costly.

The alternative way to stabilise internal prices, without the bother of paying subsidies and collecting taxes, is to destabilise the foreign exchange rate. On this plan the rate appreciates during the boom and depreciates during the slump. The simplest way to achieve this is to link the rate to an American index of wholesale prices, or a U.N.O. index of foreign trade prices. This has obvious disadvantages, but it would be much better than the policy we have pursued in the last three years.

In sum, the existence of the trade cycle presents grave difficulties in foreign trade, to which there is no perfect solution. There are three choices; to let wages and prices rise in the upswing, *on condition that they fall in the downswing ;* or, to stabilise wages and prices by subsidising imports in the up-swing, *on condition that exports are correspondingly taxed ;* or to appreciate the pound in the upswing, and depreciate in the downswing. The first of these would be resisted by the workers, and the second by the merchant community. This leaves the third as the most politically acceptable choice, though not necessarily the best economically. Whichever we choose, none is so bad as the policy which we are now actually pursuing at such great loss to the nation as a whole.

CONCLUSION

The conclusions of this chapter may be summarised as follows:

(1) Some types of foreign transaction need regulation, without prejudice to the general issue; examples are controls in the interest of defence or of infant industries, and restrictions on refugee capital.

(2) General control of trade is unnecessary if imports and exports can be kept equal without it, and without grave inconvenience; but this is seldom the case.

(3) An absolutely free rate of exchange is a nuisance; and an absolutely fixed rate of exchange is incompatible with domestic stability in countries where costs are inflexible.

(4) State planning of foreign trade would be ineffective and chaotic in the absence of international agreements prescribing the rules that planning must follow.

(5) In the long run imports and exports can be equilibrated by fixing an appropriate rate of exchange, subject to alteration as conditions change; but in the short run further controls are required, if the mobility of resources is low.

(6) Special measures to stimulate production in and trade between countries other than the U.S.A. are desirable so long as the U.S.A. has an export surplus (not covered by loans) and so long as the U.S.A. does not plan for stable employment and trade.

(7) While trade cycles last we must either let the domestic price level fluctuate with foreign prices, or let the foreign exchange rate fluctuate. We must not stabilise both domestic and external rates unless we adopt both import subsidies and export taxes.

VI

Mobility

THE efficiency of the market mechanism depends primarily on the mobility of resources, which is necessary if there is to be rapid adjustment without abnormal price movements and the hardship that they inflict. If there were perfect mobility we should never need rationing or licences, for we should never have shortages. (We could still have a general shortage if we were suffering from suppressed inflation; but the remedy for this is not rationing or licensing but disinflation.) If the quantity of money is just right, a shortage in one part of the economy must be balanced by overabundance elsewhere, and, given perfect mobility, it must rapidly disappear. It may be that the shortage is of female cotton workers in Lancashire, while the overabundance is of navvies in Kent. Perfect mobility does not require that the navvy should travel from Kent to the Lancashire mill. There is a general readjustment; he displaces someone who displaces someone else, who displaces someone else who goes into cotton. Each moves a little way until adjustment is complete. The shortage disappears when all that is wanted can be purchased freely at a reasonable price, and a reasonable price is that which corresponds to the normal average cost of production. Shortages are therefore the result of the immobility of our resources, and so also is such need as there is to use planning by direction. If we could greatly increase mobility we could eliminate all shortages, and could rely exclusively on planning by inducement. The quickest way to get rid of shortages and of licences is therefore to concentrate on immobility.

This applies as much to foreign trade as it does to domestic production. We are short of imports because we are short of exports. This is partly due to inflation, which keeps resources working for home demand, but it would not disappear at once, even if the quantity of money were right, because of immobility. Given perfect mobility, the resources released by disinflation would flow into export industries, where there is a great shortage of labour. The movement would not be direct, but would be achieved by many people making small adjustments. But in the absence of mobility disinflation creates pools of unemployment which do not necessarily reduce the shortage of labour in essential industries. The existence of immobility then comes to be used as an argument for inflation; it is no use making navvies unemployed in Kent, we are told, because there are not enough cotton operatives in Lancashire. But how are we to get more cotton operatives unless pressure is applied in other parts of the economic system? Disinflation applies pressure deliberately to what is considered least essential. The only other alternative is to carry on with the inessential while applying pressure (which in the absence of disinflation has to be the direction of labour) to industries which are themselves essential though not so essential as the export trades. Disinflation cannot be pursued smoothly unless there is a high degree of mobility; without mobility we are driven to direction of labour and of other resources.

Similarly, in the absence of mobility we cannot eliminate unemployment completely without inflation. If there were perfect mobility the 2 to 3 per cent of the population whose unemployment is frictional would disappear; there would be no frictional unemployment. But given immobility, which separates those who need work from the work of highest priority that is available, we can eliminate unemployment altogether only by providing a shortage of work everywhere, and eliminating the distinction between urgent and less urgent work. Such inflation in the labour market leads straight to the direction of labour. It is better to accept the 2 to 3 per cent and to concentrate on reducing it by eliminating immobility.

We see this problem at its worst when we consider the implications of foreign trade in a fluctuating world economy. We shall soon be in the position that about 20 per cent of the labour force depends directly on export markets. What is to happen when there is a slump and exports contract? We talk glibly of planning for full employment, but how are we to employ the workers displaced from export trades? If there were perfect mobility it would be easy; we would expand the monetary circulation and thus provide additional jobs in working for increased domestic consumption, or increased investment, or increased government service. But, with our resources as they are, such work will not be easy to organise—the equipment and the workers will not always be found together. We cannot get rid of cyclical unemployment, until we greatly increase the mobility of resources.

Equally difficult is the problem that we may call the post-re-equipment transition. At the end of the war there are great shortages of equipment to be made up, but there will come a day when the principal shortages have been made good. The back of the housing shortage will have been broken, and the demand for building labourers reduced. The mines will have been fully mechanised, and the demand both for miners and for makers of mining machinery will slacken, and so on. We cannot guarantee to each worker in each industry that his job will always be there until he dies. Full employment guarantees him some job, but not any particular job, and as conditions change many existing jobs will become redundant, and workers will be required to shift into new occupations. But, unless the workers are satisfied that new jobs will easily be found for them, they will continue, in the future as in the past, to try to resist all changes that may make the job they are doing redundant. We shall be back to restrictive practices and a low standard of living. Without easy mobility none of our problems is soluble.

If the first task of the planner is thus to ensure that there is the right amount of money in circulation, neither too much nor too little, his second priority must be to facilitate mobility. Given these two all else is easy; shortages melt away, trade balances, unemployment disappears, and so on. But if either of these two policies is defective the planner is plunged into a maze of price controls, licences and directions, in which much of efficiency and of freedom is easily lost.

The way to facilitate mobility is to plan the location of industry, to facilitate the acquisition of skills and to plan the wage structure.

LOCATION

The need to facilitate mobility is only one aspect of the problem of location, which we must examine in its widest setting.

The truth is that the market mechanism, acting through prices, is wholly incompetent to procure the correct location of industry. For example, if we are considering the disadvantages of allowing large towns to grow, such factors as traffic congestion do appear in prices, but inferior health conditions reflect less adequately and military considerations hardly reflect at all. Prices reflect wages, but wages are bad guides to location, for, wages being sticky, the wage differentials between towns where there is heavy unemployment and towns where there is not are not as wide as a free market would require. Similarly, the prices of services provided by public authorities do not adequately reflect social costs, with the result that new industries causing a town to expand do not pay the full extra costs they impose by way of extra schools, hospitals and so on, while in depressed areas, as excess capacity develops the rates tend to rise instead of to fall. Again, there is nothing in prices to reflect the disadvantage, in terms of mobility and thus also of unemployment and human misery, of having an entire region specialised to a particular trade, and dependent on its fortunes. Nor do prices adequately check the cumulative or multiplier processes at work in location. If by some chance accident a big factory migrates from one town to another (not necessarily only because the manager's wife wishes to be near London) cumulative forces are set up. The loss of purchasing power in the town it has left reduces the markets for firms that remain, and causes some to move, their movement in turn driving away still more. And in the town to which it has moved there is a cumulative upswing. Prices are supposed to check these tendencies through rents and quasi-rents, but these are sticky. This is why when a town starts to run down, it may die, and its industries transfer to some other town which grows rapidly, although in fact there is very little to choose between the two towns, and certainly not enough to justify the big differences caused by the cumulative process. (This recalls the similar deflationary process in export trade; those who say that there is no difference between foreign and domestic trade are right —both may cause serious waste and hardship if unregulated, and through the same processes.) The fact is simply that the price mechanism is a bad guide to location. This is certainly one of the most necessary spheres for planning.

But, of course, it is not true that *any* planning is better than none. There are important issues in deciding what to plan, how to plan, and where to plan.

Only mobile industries should be planned, that is to say only industries that are not tied to particular locations, either because they are service industries or because they need particular raw materials or types of labour or water supplies or other services that can be provided elsewhere only at much higher social cost. When we undertake to plan location we are assuming that there exists a large number of these mobile industries, sufficient to give us the diversification that we need. No one can foresee whether this will prove to be true, for no one knows what types of industry are most likely to be expanding in this country in the next twenty-five years, nor what their locational needs must be.

It is this that makes the technique of location planning so important. When areas are scheduled for restriction, it is important to restrict only the mobile industries, which will not be gravely handicapped if they locate elsewhere; other industries should have freedom to locate where they please. And when we are seeking to develop particular regions it is better to proceed by inducement than by direction. We have rightly decided that the best way to encourage new industries is to provide the basic services that they require, especially using the happy invention of the trading estate, and to subsidise such services if necessary. If industry will not come to an area even when special efforts are made to reduce the cost of working there, it is dangerous to direct it there, for there must be something basically wrong with the area.

What should guide the choice of areas? Military factors seem to have been dominant in selecting the London area for discouragement, with almost universal approval, but there is less agreement on the choice of areas for encouragement. Nearly everyone agrees that the old special areas should be given new industries, because people and services are already there, even though it is agreed that it is a bad proposition ever to 'freeze' the current geographical distribution of the population. Actually, the war has solved most of this problem; given a full employment policy the special areas will soon have enough industries to provide work for all. The sharpest dispute has been over the new industrial areas which must arise with the growth of population: should new industries be dispersed throughout the countryside, providing extra opportunities of employment for the families of agricultural workers, or should they be concentrated in new towns? For the moment the 'romantics' have won, with the aid of the shortage of agricultural labour; the rural atmosphere is to be preserved. It is in any case doubtful whether dispersal could ever get far; factories like to be close together, where they can share good basic industrial facilities; there are some industries which could survive without subsidy dispersed in lonely rural isolation, but they are not very numerous.

To facilitate mobility we must add to these considerations the need to diversify regions, so that if a major industry slumps its workers can be easily absorbed into other industries close at hand. This means that no major industry subject to drastic fluctuations should be confined in a single region, and that no region should be dependent on some such industry. The major industries subject to drastic fluctuation are the export industries, especially textiles, coal, iron and steel and some branches of engineering. We need to move some of the textile factories of Lancashire and Yorkshire into regions not now so dependent on exports, e.g. into the south, and into some of the new towns; to move some of the domestic industries into their place, and some more into regions now too dependent on coal, on shipbuilding, or on export engineering. We have not started to tackle this problem yet, but it will stare us starkly in the face with the first slump in foreign trade. It is indeed staring us in the face now, with the boom in foreign trade and the shortage of labour in export trades, which is partly due to their geographical concentration. At first we tried to avoid facing it, but the dwindling of foreign reserves put an end to that, and now we are trying to meet it by half-hearted importation of foreign labour. This is inevitable; as industry is now located the quickest way to fill the gaps is selective immigration, and we cannot afford to wait on slower methods. But the slump will come, and cannot be ignored or met by expelling foreign labour. It can be met only by so dispersing export industries amongst those catering for home demand, that it becomes easy to affect rapid transfers from one to the other. Here we have not even made the preliminary survey of what is involved, but until we achieve this diversification all glib talk of guaranteeing full employment is so much foolishness.

Planning location is a very difficult job, and one in which we are sure to make many mistakes. Here, as much as anywhere else, policy must be flexible, criticism must be welcomed, and there must be full opportunities for appeal. Planners know what has happened in the past, but they cannot foresee the future. The major industries of today will be forgotten tomorrow. In twenty-five years Britain's greatness will depend on industries which are only now germinating, and whose progress depends on the freedom allowed to men of initiative. In this respect our problems are much more complicated than those of newer countries because it is we who pioneer the new, while they have only to imitate. At this stage of their development Russia and Eastern European countries are merely establishing industries that Western Europe and the U.S.A. have fully explored long ago; they have fewer mistakes to make, and their planning, however rigid, cannot do as much damage as would rigid planning in this country.

SKILL

A much less difficult problem is that of facilitating the acquisition of skills, so that the unemployed may be absorbed easily into new trades. In olden days a long apprenticeship was thought necessary, and so it still is, in some jobs; but in many others a man may now learn as much in a well organised training centre in six weeks or in three months or in six months as he learnt before in four years of haphazard apprenticeship. This is now recognised, and many government training centres have accordingly been established.

The difficulty that remains is the unwillingness of some trade unions to accept newcomers who have not had the traditional apprenticeship. This is based often on real concern for standards; but as often it is based on fear. There are many hangovers from the days of mass unemployment, and this is one of them. Once the workers are persuaded, by experience, that, whatever may happen, British governments will always have the maintenance of full employment as one of their first objectives,

F

this sort of fear will disappear. But we must not be surprised if centuries of hard experience are not rejected overnight. Fortunately the industries in which objection to 'dilution' is a problem are not numerous, and this is not now one of the major obstacles to mobility.

CONDITIONS OF WORK

Wages and other conditions of work play a smaller role in determining mobility than is usually thought. If the quantity of money were right a shortage of labour in some trades would always be balanced by unemployment in others, and, given no geographical obstacles to mobility, the unemployment would quickly be absorbed even though wages were no higher in the trades where labour was short than in trades where labour was abundant. It is only where there is inflation, and jobs can be had in all trades, that it becomes necessary sharply to differentiate in wages and conditions between jobs that are essential and those that are not.

It so happens, in contemporary Britain, that the differentiation works the wrong way. The essential jobs, where labour is now most scarce, are to a large extent jobs in which labour was overabundant between the wars. It is not merely that wages in these jobs have been low—that can be remedied overnight; it is also that the conditions of workplaces are unfavourable—buildings are old, and welfare accommodation poor—and, still worse, that the record of these industries, in terms of unemployment and prospects of security, is so bad that workers have lost confidence in these industries. These difficulties cannot be overcome rapidly. We can raise wages, make a start on improving physical conditions, and swear to maintain full employment, but it will be long before the status of these industries is restored to a level at which recruits flow in easily.

This is also a reminder that wages are not the only or the dominating attraction to a job. But, once we have levelled up the physical conditions and wiped out the memory of insecurity, they come into their own again. They are important both positively and negatively; positively in that superior wages do attract, and negatively in that superior wages are needed to offset unpleasant conditions of labour—work that is dirty or hot or monotonous. In conditions of full employment jobs of equal skill must be paid equal wages, with allowances one way or the other for differences in the pleasantness of the work. To achieve this position we shall need in this country a radical overhaul of the structure of wages, for the existing structure belongs to an economy of mass unemployment rather than to the nineteen-fifties. The dirty jobs are paid less than the clean jobs, of equal skill; many unskilled wages are too high, relatively to those of craftsmen; the wages of women and of boys are appropriate only to the old conditions when women and boys were in surplus supply; wages in consumer goods industries and services are too high in relation to the producer goods industries; methods of payment do not offer sufficient incentive; and so on. Until these matters are righted many essential industries will continue to find it difficult to attract away from the inessential all the labour they need.

This is the case for the planning of wages. What is needed is not to 'freeze' wages, but on the contrary to raise a great number of classes of wages which are now too low. But this is a task which can succeed only if those wages that are not in the priority classes can be held while the adjustment is effected.

In planning to leave behind the days of violent boom and slump, in which unemployment forced wages to adjust to relative shortages, we leave behind the days when each trade union could safely be left to try to get as much as it could for itself. Wages must now be subject to central control. But who is to control the centre? In a democratic country wages cannot be controlled without the full consent and cooperation not only of the union leaders, but also of the rank and file, and this means that we cannot even embark on solving this problem until it is widely understood by the rank and file, and until the will to solve it exists. To frame machinery that would examine each wage claim in relation to the general level of wages in the public interest is the task of a moment. But what we need now is rather to concentrate on the educational job of getting the rank and file to understand why, in a full employment economy, what matters is not the absolute level of wages, but the relation of each wage to the general level. Naturally, this proposition will not be accepted until the workers are convinced that the government is earnestly planning for equality in other ways, is determined on full employment, and has the activities of capitalists well under control, and since all these things take time to demonstrate, there is little prospect of achieving a planned wage structure in the near future.

We cannot, in a word, solve the social problems left by centuries of *laisser-faire* in a year or two. In dealing with a wages structure, as with location, the best we can do is to begin to lay the foundations. It will be many years before the economy achieves flexibility. The corollaries of this are that the immediate urgencies of labour shortage in essential industries will have to be met largely by immigration; and that planning by direction, in the shape of rationing and licensing, which is due principally to immobility, will remain with us for some time yet. But the fact that these tasks will take us long to fulfil only makes it all the more urgent to work upon them now.

We have, in particular, been very foolish not to make full use of immigration, as other countries have done, to man up essential industries. We could have restored the output of coal to the pre-war level, and not only in this way reduced the adverse balance of payments and avoided our own fuel crisis, but also made a great contribution to European recovery, and to the comfort of the scores of millions on the continent whose wintry miseries in the past three years have been due to our nonchalant failure seriously to tackle the manpower problem in coal; we have a lot to answer for here. We could also have manned up agriculture, textiles, and other essential industries. In 1938 more than a quarter of our exports consisted of coal and of cotton and woollens. If we had the same volume of these exports today that we had then we should have no adverse balance, and we could have achieved this simply by allowing in about 200,000 workers, on condition that they went to work in essential industries. If we had done this we should now be able to import more food, and would be free of rationing and of other irksome controls of consumption. How small the margin has been very few people realise. 200,000 is only about 1 per cent of our working population, and it is only for lack of this 1 per cent that we have exposed ourselves to so much stress, and imposed upon other nations so much hardship. We could have got all the workers we needed very easily in 1946; they would have been glad to have the opportunity to come, in spite of the over-crowded housing that was all that we could offer, knowing that in all other respects they would have exactly the same pay and conditions as their fellow British workers, and that they would have been much better off here than where they were. It is not so easy now; other nations, more sensible than we, have already skimmed the cream. But it would still be possible, if we wished to do it. The real reason why we have not done it is that neither the government nor the public has sufficiently realised the importance of mobility. We have talked of the need for extra production without seeming to realise that it is more important to produce some things than to produce others, and that what we really need is more of some and less of others. So long as the real nature of our problem has been hidden, false nationalism and other obstacles have triumphed over common sense. How to get labour into the places where it is most urgently needed—that is the first function of an economic system. When we realise this, all our problems will be solved; but till then we shall continue to waste our resources, and to inflict miseries both upon ourselves and upon our neighbours.

Once we have got through the big readjustments demanded by the war and reconversion, the mobility of labour may well prove a much less difficult problem than it is now fashionable to think. Many people suggest that full employment makes labour less willing to move, but there is no evidence for this. On the contrary, full employment is more usually associated with an excessive turnover of labour, and it is not full employment but the universal shortage of houses that is at present holding down mobility. When there is a sufficient surplus of houses for a worker to feel confident of getting a house wherever he may move, the problem in full employment is more likely to be that labour is too mobile than that it is too little mobile. If by that time the wage structure has been revised to make equally difficult jobs equally remunerative; and if we have learnt the secret of having neither too much money nor too little, so that shortage in one part of the economy is always balanced by equivalent surpluses elsewhere (and *vice versa*); then the supply of labour should prove sufficiently responsive to marginal changes in the demands of different industries and places.

CONCLUSION

We may summarise as follows:

(1) The smoothness with which the market economy functions depends on the extent to which resources are mobile; it is immobility that necessitates planning by direction.

(2) *Laisser-faire* leads to incorrect location; location must be planned in the social interest, and, in particular, in such a way as to facilitate easy mobility between trades.

(3) The acquisition of new skills must be made as easy as is possible.

(4) The wage structure needs to be planned in order that essential trades in which there is a shortage of labour should be made more attractive than other trades.

(5) Monetary equilibrium is also essential to mobility, so that the supply of labour may be responsive to marginal changes in the demands of different industries and places. The distribution of resources is governed principally by the distribution of the flow of money, which is disturbed equally by inflation and by deflation.

(6) The achievement of a high level of mobility is a long job; meanwhile our immediate problems must be solved by selective immigration.

VII

The Social Control of Business

IN the free market economy the activities of business men are
controlled by the pressure of competition. It is competition that
forces them to follow demand, competition that enforces
efficiency, and competition that keeps profits low. In this, as in
other respects, the market economy cannot do its job if it is
checked by inflation, for inflation creates a sellers' market,
removes the control of demand, encourages waste, and causes
profits to rise faster than wages. In this, as in all else, the first
principle of planning is to have neither too little nor too
much money in circulation.

If the level of monetary circulation is just right profits will
be 'normal', that is they will be no more than is needed to
induce business men to offer full employment. The word
'normal' carries no moral significance. Socialists think that the
level of profits that is necessary to ensure full employment is
too high, and gives to business men too large a share of the
national income for what they do. They are then tempted to
reduce profits by raising wages. But, as we have already seen
in Chapter II, raising the general level of money wages merely
raises the general level of prices. And if prices are controlled
and wages raised relatively to them we both cause unemployment and distort the structure of production. The smooth way
to increase wages relatively to profits is to put low taxes on
wage earners and high taxes on large and on unearned incomes.
The income tax is a wonderful invention because it does the
same job that the trade unions wish to do without the evil
results, for the simple reason that it does not enter into costs,
and so has only small effects on entrepreneurial decisions as to
employment. And also, more fundamentally, the way to reduce
profits, in the long run, is to ensure equality of opportunity.
If everyone in the community had the same sort of opportunities

of becoming an entrepreneur, business men would not earn
more than anyone else. The way to control profits is to subject
business men to as much competition as possible.

These wider issues we have already discussed. What concerns
us in this chapter is only what happens within the framework of
normal profits; for even on this narrower ground the claims of
competition do not pass unchallenged. Its enemies assert first
that it is not fully effective in spurring business men to efficiency,
secondly that their response to it is frequently on the contrary
to behave wastefully, thirdly that competition is ruinous, and
fourthly that it is in any case self-destructive.

PRODUCTIVITY

Efficiency depends in the first place upon research, and upon
its application. Competition stimulates research, but since only
the largest firms can afford fundamental research, the result,
in some industries, is to increase the advantages of large firms
and to diminish the prospects of competition; and in other
industries predominantly small scale, the result is that little
research occurs. One remedy for both of these is cooperative
research, which has been officially sponsored and assisted in
this country for the past thirty years. Everyone agrees that
cooperative research should be on a larger scale, and many
think that every firm should be made to contribute, since all
may benefit, and that as much emphasis as possible should be
placed on cooperative at the expense of private research, so
that new knowledge may be made available to all.

The imperfection of competition also reveals itself in the
coexistence of firms differing widely in efficiency. Doubtless
there is a tendency, in the long run, for the more efficient to
drive the less efficient out of business, but it is even better, and
may be quicker, to increase the efficiency of the latter by instruc-
tion. In agriculture, normally a most competitive industry, no one
believes that competition alone is adequate to ensure efficiency;
there is, on the contrary, in every country an elaborate system
of advisory services placed at the farmer's disposal, and sub-
sidised from public funds. Industry needs such services no less.

We have selected here only two of the services which a
' Development Council ' might usefully supervise, and for which

funds may justifiably be levied compulsorily upon industries. It is not, naturally, easy to get such councils accepted; the bigger and more efficient firms see no gain to themselves, but only the expense of levies and the prospect of more effective competition; the smaller firms often do not feel the need for the services they are to be offered; and existing associations resent the intrusion of new bodies. It may seem useless to force upon industries services which they have determined to resist; but, once the deed is done, and the services become available, resistance frequently ends, and the new institution is accepted, and if it proves its worth, is eventually proudly cherished.

We have become aware recently how much productivity could be increased with existing plant and labour, simply by improving the organisation of work in the factory. There is partly a matter of improving management, through the training schemes and the advisory services of development councils. But it is also partly a matter of securing the agreement of workers to discontinue restrictive practices, tacit or expressed.

Production would increase if workers would work harder. This is quite a different issue. There is no case for trying to force people to work harder, or to work longer hours. Doubtless if they did they would have a higher standard of living, but they would also have more wear and tear and less leisure, and the purpose of life is not to wear oneself out in toil for material standards. Doubtless, too, if full employment were removed, and the insecurity and fear of dismissal hung once more over the workers' heads, they could be driven in many directions. But it is not consistent with democracy to force people to have a higher material standard by holding a whip of fear over their heads. If full employment causes productivity to fall, then this is part of the case for full employment, and not of the case against it; for it emphasises that it is only in full employment that the workers get a real choice between extra income and extra leisure. All the speeches urging the workers to work harder are so much wasted breath. The fact is that the workers on the whole do not like the sort of jobs they have to do, and when they get the chance to take things easy, which is presented by higher hourly earnings and by full employment, they take it. Those of us who have 'cushy' jobs—politicians, professors, clergymen, newspaper editors and the like—may think that this is wrong; but it is only natural, and no amount of preaching is going to change it.

The real issue is not to get people to work more or harder, but to get their agreement to working more effectively. Through fear of unemployment the workers have imposed many restrictions—on the number of machines each worker shall tend, on the introduction of new machines, on the use of incentive wage systems, on the maximum daily output per worker (usually only by tacit agreement) and so on. These will disappear when the workers are fully convinced that full employment has come to stay, but not till then. Those who grumble because our productivity is low should determine all the more to maintain full employment, which alone in due course will make possible the most effective use of our resources.

Progress in this sphere depends also on the internal atmosphere of the business unit. The worker will give his best only if he identifies himself with his working unit, and has towards it sentiments of pride and of loyalty. This is largely a matter of the personal relations between management and managed, but it depends also to some extent on securing to workers some participation in management. The importance of this is both exaggerated and underestimated. In a large firm the vast majority can play little part in management; the workers may elect delegates, but the workers are by definition so numerous and the delegates so few that the election interests only the active minority. What is missing in the large firm is personal contact between management and managed, and for this participation in management through delegates is but a poor substitute. On the other hand, it can be better than nothing, especially if a large measure of decentralisation is possible, so that the units of decision are numerous; then there can be numerous opportunities for worker participation, and correspondingly more delegates. Experience shows that, once the atmosphere is right, all questions of internal discipline, punctuality, absenteeism and so on can safely be left to the workers themselves to regulate, through their committees, and that there is no part of the managerial problem which does not become easier if the workers are taken into full consultation. There have also been striking results in the U.S.A. from giving the workers a fixed share of sales, basing this on the fact that the share of wages in production changes very little, either in short periods, or over many years; when the workers know that they get a fixed percentage of what they produce (the appropriate figure varies from industry to industry, according to the importance of raw materials and of amortisation of plant), however much or however little they may produce, their attitude to their work becomes very different from what it is when they are working for fixed wages. In this and other ways we may seek to create a sense of community and responsibility in the industrial unit, so that men may take a full pride in the work that they do.

In all this we are still at the stage of experiment, and the best contribution that a government can make is to experiment in its own nationalised undertakings and so try to give a lead to private industry. This is not a field where legislation is very helpful, since success depends primarily on good personal relations. Moreover if worker participation in management really increases productivity, the firms that practise it will, in competition, make headway at the expense of those that do not; and, in full employment, the reluctant firms will be ground between this competition and the strong bargaining pressure of workers seeking in collective agreements to secure fuller participation. An enormous increase in productivity is possible as soon as the workers become interested in this subject and start bringing pressure to bear on the less efficient firms to improve their methods.

In this sphere the major responsibility rests with the trade unions. The lead they have given to the working classes in the past has been restrictive and destructive. They have sought to protect vested interests because the insecurity of the economic system gave such protection the first priority. If we can demonstrate that full employment has really come to stay, and also that extra production will not be used just to make the rich richer, the engines can be reversed. The rank and file can learn to take a pride in output, and energies now distorted and frustrated can be released and directed to the great task of abolishing poverty by producing more. Trade unionists can become authorities not only on wages and conditions, but also on managerial techniques and on productivity, and can bring their great pressure to bear on inefficient firms that are wasting men's labour. Collective agreements may come to include important clauses binding the employer to use up-to-date methods. Joint production councils, which are in danger of being no more than a drag on industry as long as working class leaders are not really interested in questions of production and have little to contribute on them, can spring to life, and really do the job for which they are designed. We are still a long way from this, but it must clearly be our objective.

WASTEFUL COMPETITION

In all that we have discussed so far, competition is working in the right direction; that is to say, however slowly, it is working on the side of efficiency. It may, however, work the other way when markets are imperfect. For then the seller, instead of trying to sell as cheaply as possible, may rely instead on differentiating his product from that of his rivals. This differentiation may be costly. The consumer is inconvenienced if the absence of standardisation makes it difficult to secure spare parts and other accessories easily; marketing costs are high; firms are too numerous and too small; and factory costs are too high. Competition works well if it encourages more people to produce a standard article, but it begins to be costly when, through market imperfection, it results in differentiation of product.

There are forces at work in the market that restrain this process. If any manufacturer thinks that standardisation will greatly reduce cost, he is at liberty to take the plunge—it is this that made millionaires of men like Henry Ford. And if it is an article in daily common use, the growth of large scale retailing—the Woolworths, the multiple shops and so on—provides an outlet for orders by the million. With most of the things in common use the market forces are strong enough to exploit all the economies of mass production. Where the case is more doubtful is with articles that are as yet within the reach only of the middle and upper classes, where there is good technical reason to think that costs would fall greatly if production were standardised. The motor car is an outstanding English example, but there are also a few others, such as refrigerators or television sets.

There is also a case against standardisation, namely that it puts a straight jacket upon an industry, and checks the speed at which new improvements can be introduced. This applies equally to 'utility' specifications, and to proposals that Government departments should place large bulk orders for resale to retailers; though in truth no more harm is done by government standardisation than is done by the standardisation imposed by securing a mammoth Woolworth order, provided that the government's specification is as responsive to changing conditions as is Woolworth's. The moral is that compulsory standardisation should be applied sparingly, and flexibly, in such a way that new ideas and new designs can still be introduced and find scope for experimental use and improvement. Standardisation should not be applied where technical progress is fairly rapid, and should not be applied where it may have adverse effects on export trade. The best agency for deciding when to effect compulsory standardisation is a Development Council representing all sections of the industry and the public.

It is the absence of standardisation that causes excessive expenditure on advertising and sales promotion, and if the root cause is controlled there is no need for special action to deal with effects. Where compulsory standardisation is desirable and is applied, further control of sales promotion activities will not be necessary. Where standardisation is not desirable it is *ipso facto* desirable that the existence of a wide range of varieties should be made known, and therefore expenditure on sales promotion is in the public interest. If special restrictions of sales promotion are considered desirable, they should be left to voluntary arrangement at the instance of Development Councils.

Absence of standardisation is also the secret of waste in wholesale and retail distribution. The large organisations in distribution, such as the multiple shops and the co-ops, flourish by concentrating on a limited range of articles and doing a big trade in them; while the inefficiency of some of the small retailers is due to their trying to cover too wide a range. Progress in distribution will occur both through the further extension of large scale retailing at the expense of small scale and through the improvement of the latter. Experience in the U.S.A. shows that the key to the success of small scale retailing is cooperation; taking the form of cooperation between a number of independent retailers and a wholesaler to ensure the fullest benefits of standardisation and bulk-buying; this system has worked wonders in the U.S.A. for the small retailer, and could do the same here. But retailers will not adopt it so long as there is available to them the alternative but illusory protection of resale price maintenance, which, in so far as it fixes a minimum price below which goods must not be sold, has been one of the principal sources of waste in retailing. This system should be prohibited by law. The small retailers would then have to set to work to improve their efficiency by legitimate means, especially by cooperation in buying and merchandising, and one of the restraints which now prevent the expansion of efficient forms of retailing would be removed. The special interest of socialists is of course in the further expansion of the consumers' cooperative movement. This movement is disappointing in the sense that the trade it does is not commensurate with its membership of over 10 millions, for the simple reason that the members do not find their own shops competitive except in a small part of the retail trade. This should be a standing challenge to the movement, but it is not, because the leaders of the movement seem more anxious to increase the number of names in membership books than to widen the range of goods which existing members find competitive. To the socialist the reform of distribution must mean first the reform of the consumers' cooperative movement. This is a difficult task, and to discuss it fully would take us beyond our terms of reference, which is the sphere of government planning. We can say only that if the movement cannot be reformed in such a way that it becomes competitive and secures the larger part of retail trade, the Government must look to the development and extension of other forms of mass retailing in the spheres where the cooperative movement is failing.

RUINOUS COMPETITION

The general level of profits, we have already seen, depends not on competition but on the circulation of money. Profits are low if there is less than full employment, high if there is inflation, and normal at full employment. Competition cannot be ruinous either to profits or to wages so long as the monetary circulation is right.

This, however, refers only to general levels. Competition c⁀n be ruinous to particular groups in the sense that it causes their earnings to fall far below the general level; in doing this it must raise the earnings of other groups, but the fact that others are better off is not of much consolation to the particular group ruined by competition.

This phenomenon of ruinous competition, driving some earnings below the general level, is the result of immobility. If resources were not immobile, their owners would not remain in the group that is subjected to this strain; they would rapidly disperse elsewhere, and as the supply to this group diminished, earnings would return to normal. It is only when resources are very immobile and subjected to a large adverse change that the phenomenon of ruinous competition appears. Between 1920 and 1939 many of the old staple industries of Britain suffered this fate, especially coal, cotton, steel, shipbuilding, and agriculture.

If the immobile resources are left to their fate they will eventually disperse elsewhere—the more rapidly if the circulation of money is adequate to provide full employment for all (the long drawn out process in Britain between the wars was due less to immobility and more to the absence of a full employment policy). But if they are very immobile, special measures are required. In the first place, we can no longer tolerate the spectacle of citizens subjected to years of agonising ruin simply because demand for their services has altered, without doing something to bring their agony to an end. In the second place, it is wasteful for resources to remain where they are not very valuable, and we should facilitate their transfer. And in the third place a long drawn out agony is literally ruinous to an industry. It may be that only 10 per cent of resources is in excess, but the whole industry makes losses, funds are not set aside for renewing and improving the 90 per cent of plant that is needed, and the industry falls behind technically; at the same time young men avoid the industry; its age structure is distorted; and it acquires an evil reputation which works against new recruitment when the state of surplus gives way to that of shortage. All our old industries, now short of labour and burdened with obsolete equipment, are suffering from having been too long left to the agonies of ruinous competition.

The industry's own remedy in this situation is to end competition. If supplies are restricted by quota, prices can be fixed high enough to give reasonable profits and wages; they can even be fixed high enough to give abnormal profits, though in practice there is no danger of this. The objection to this solution of the problem is that it does not deal with the fundamental cause of trouble, which is the excess of immobile resources. What is needed is a scheme to facilitate mobility, and though it is justifiable in the meantime to prevent earnings from falling to ruinous levels, the emphasis should be on mobility, and protection should be the subsidiary and temporary part of the scheme.

MONOPOLY

At the other extreme we get the case where a particular group is able to receive abnormal earnings, which, if there is neither inflation nor deflation, must be at the expense of the rest of society. This again is due to barriers to mobility. The abnormality may be temporary. If there is a sudden increase in demand or fall in supply the group may receive abnormal earnings until such time as extra resources are drawn in and prices and earnings fall to normal level. If the commodity is essential we may then have price control and rationing, and, if we are sensible, also special inducements to facilitate mobility and restore supply to a normal level. In a competitive market supply will always expand, until demand is satisfied at a price equal to normal cost of production. We call monopoly the case where additional resources are prevented from flowing into the group and bringing earnings to a normal level.

The normal way to deal with monopoly is to remove the barriers to the flow of resources on which it depends. Where monopoly is due to denial of finance to competitors, the remedy is a finance corporation. Where it is due to securing price discrimination against rival suppliers, the remedy is to outlaw discrimination. If it is due to abuse of patents, to trade boycotts, to exclusive agreements, or other loopholes in the law, the remedy is to reform the law. This has been one of the purposes of American anti-trust legislation, and this part of the anti-trust law has been highly successful. In this country we are proceeding more slowly; we are not passing general legislation outlawing monopoly practices, but shall investigate each industry, and make orders applicable only to one industry at a time. This slowness is due in part to believing that monopoly can be conquered simply by publicity; and that therefore when a practice is outlawed in any one industry business men will abandon it in all others without waiting for a commission to get round to them industry by industry. Such faith seems somewhat naive; sooner or later we too, in the U.K., will pass general laws outlawing monopoly practices.

But not all monopoly can be dealt with by changes in the law. For example, where monopoly is based on owning all the supplies of a mineral the law can do nothing to make competition. So also where the monopoly is based on the economies of large scale production. There are even cases where monopoly should be encouraged. This is so wherever it is thought that unified control is necessary in order to minimise costs; and also in a few cases where the market is small and the risks so great that no one will provide a supply unless given at least temporary protection.

Where competition cannot be enforced, or where monopoly is actually desirable, what we need is not attempts to promote competition, but the control of monopoly. This is done by legislation fixing prices or profits, laying down the conditions of supply, and establishing a controlling tribunal. It is not essential that monopolies be nationalised, and whether they be nationalised or not, the same machinery of control is needed in order to protect the public. Of such machinery there are many examples in all democratic countries, where there is long experience of public utility control. Democrats make much song and dance about monopoly, but to deal with monopoly is one of the easiest problems of planning.

CONCLUSION

We may summarise as follows:

(1) Efficiency demands research, advisory services, and some measure of standardisation. In Britain the best way to work for each of these is through Development Councils.

G

(2) Efficiency depends on enlisting the pride and cooperation of all the workers in a business unit. Government can give a lead by experimenting in nationalised concerns with worker participation in management and with new forms of wage contract.

(3) Ruinous competition should be prevented where resources are very immobile, and deliberate dispersal should be pursued.

(4) Monopolistic practices that prevent the free flow of resources should be outlawed.

(5) Monopolies based on the economies of large scale production, or temporary monopolies granted for special reasons, should be controlled as to price, profits and conditions of sale.

VIII

Nationalisation

THE nationalisation of industry is not essential to planning; a government can do nearly anything it wants to do by way of controlling industry without resorting to nationalisation, as in Nazi Germany. Nationalisation is merely one of the ways of achieving ends; better for some ends, and not so good for others. We may begin by classifying the reasons for which nationalisation has been advocated.

First, socialists have wished the state to confiscate the property of the rich. But nationalisation is not confiscation. In Britain when we nationalise we pay the owners the full value of their property so that they are no less rich after nationalisation than before. This is done for the excellent reason that everything is not being nationalised at the same time. If one is nationalising only certain industries it would be unfair to confiscate the property of their capitalists while leaving all other capitalists untouched. And it would also be unwise because other capitalists who expected their own turn to come would withdraw as much capital as possible from industries on the nationalisation list, while there was yet time, to the detriment of the efficiency of these industries. If the fear of future nationalisation is not to stop the wheels of industry, capitalists must know that they will be treated fairly when their turn comes, so that they may continue to keep their industries going until the state gets round to them. Compensation must not be unfair, and if it errs, should, for this reason, err on the generous side. Confiscation proceeds not by nationalisation, but by taxation, especially death duties and capital levies, which should be pursued whether nationalisation takes place or not.

Secondly, in recent years in this country nationalisation has come to be thought of as necessary where capitalists have not been putting enough money into an industry, as into the British coal, cotton, agricultural or steel industries between

1920 and 1939. Actually the real reason why capitalists put little money into those industries in that period was that the demand for their products was relatively small, for special reasons. If the British Government had owned the coal industry, or cotton, or the land in the 1920s and 1930s it would have been just as reluctant to invest new capital in them as were the private capitalists. There is, after all, no chronic tendency of capitalists not to invest; they put their money where prospects are brightest, and poured plenty into the land or coal in the years before 1920 before conditions abroad cast their blight upon the prospects of these staple industries. It is not necessary to nationalise steel or the land in order to get capital invested in them. All the capital that is wanted will flow in if prospects are bright, and if the government wants capital to flow in even though prospects are uncertain (a decision which it should not take lightly) it has only to guarantee the market for the product, or to guarantee debenture payments, or, as it has done in the cotton industry, to offer an outright subsidy.

Thirdly, nationalisation has been advocated by socialists who have objected to the proletariat working for private employers who own the means of production. In olden days when the scale of production was very small the workers could own their own instruments of production, and it is much pleasanter to work for oneself than to work for someone else. But nationalisation does very little to solve this problem. What early socialists demanded was not nationalisation but cooperative production— the mines would be handed over to the miners as their own property, to run them as they pleased on a cooperative basis. British socialists have now rejected this conception; the mines, or any other nationalised property, are to belong to the public, who will employ the miners, and the essential relation is not changed by the change of ownership. It is of course very desirable that in nationalised enterprises the workers shall participate fully in management, and be treated with the fullest human dignity, but this is just as necessary in private industry, and is not, in fact, any easier to achieve in nationalised industries than it is in private industries, given in each case that the owner of the property, public or private, is retaining and protecting certain rights. We have to do everything that we can, in public and private industry, to revolutionise the status of working people; but if we rest too much of the case for nationalisation on this ground we shall only be bitterly disappointed.

We come on to more solid ground where nationalisation is advocated for an industry where efficiency depends on unitary control. A good example of this is the ownership of mineral rights. When mining rights are owned by thousands of small landowners, each of whom may grant a mining licence to whatever company he pleases, the working of the mineral underground is seldom performed economically; companies are too small, and their boundaries bear no relation to geological conditions. There is a similar case for *land* nationalisation, where the existing pattern of ownership is causing farms to be uneconomic in size and shape, or frustrating town or country planning. The telephone service is also another example, because of the advantage of having all the subscribers in an area on the same system; and so is the generation of electricity, because of the advantage of pooling reserves. Still another important class are industries where standardisation would bring substantial economies, where such standardisation is being frustrated by the existing pattern of ownership. Of these the most important example in this country is *the motor car industry*. Also in this category we must include industries where excessive use of selling or buying agents by rival firms causes great waste, as is alleged to be the case with *insurance* in this country, and with *the marketing of agricultural produce* in many backward countries.

Unitary control is not the same as nationalisation; it becomes part of the case for nationalisation only because it involves monopoly, and then it merges into the general case for nationalising monopolies, whether they are based upon a need for unitary control or not, because it is desirable that monopolies be subjected to public control. Nationalisation is not the only possible form of control. Monopolies can be controlled by setting up a tribunal to fix their prices, or by controlling their profits, or laying down conditions of service as has been done here and elsewhere for generations with gas, railways, and other public utilities. Neither does nationalisation even make it possible to evade having to have these types of control, because it is just as necessary to have these controls over public as over private monopolies. The only thing that nationalisation adds is the right to appoint the directors. This is an important right, and one that it is necessary for the state to be able to exercise over all industries that play an important part in the economy. This is a vague phrase admittedly; it applies not to consumer goods industries, but to monopolistic industries which supply services widely used by other industries, such as railways, *steel*, *banking*, or *chemicals*. It is not for nothing that the capitalists in these industries are usually looked up to by other capitalists as the great lords of capitalism, and given positions of responsibility wherever spokesmen are needed to represent the general interests of the class. These positions wield great power, and it is right that those who hold them should be nominated by the public and be answerable to the public.

In so far as the purpose of nationalisation is the control of monopoly, nationalisation need not itself be monopolistic, except in those cases where unitary control is essential to efficiency. An industry can be controlled by nationalising a part of it, just as private monopolists frequently exercise leadership and control of an industry even though their own firms may supply well under half the output. This is important first because it makes it unnecessary to try to draw the line very precisely in defining the industry to be nationalised. The important thing is to nationalise all or enough of the big firms to secure control. Neither does it matter if the firms one nationalises have interests in processes or industries outside the range of special interest. There is no reason why these should not be kept even if it means participating in other industries which are largely in private hands. There is a case for having some private firms in industries mainly nationalised, to act as a check on the efficiency of the public firms, and to provide an outlet for ideas which the public firms might suppress (this is particularly important in a country dependent on foreign trade). And equally there is a good case for public firms in many industries that are largely in private hands, to serve similarly as a yardstick and as an opportunity for experiments. The government should have power to start or to buy firms by private contract in any industry for this purpose. Partial nationalisation has many advantages over complete nationalisation of an industry.

It is also desirable that, except where there are special advantages in unitary control, the public sector of an industry should be decentralised as much as possible, to the extent of being administered by several independent corporations instead of by a single corporation. There is a case for having several B.B.Cs instead of one, and several Coal Boards. Decentralisation is desirable in the interest of efficiency, because enormous corporations are difficult to administer from a single centre. It is also necessary if the participation of workers in management is to be real, for if the decisions are all made at the centre very few can participate; the greater the number of points at which decisions are made, the greater the number of workers that can be drawn in, and the greater the sense of participation and of loyalty. This is specially important because it is the duty of public corporations to give a lead in promoting a new atmosphere of cooperation in industry. And thirdly, decentralisation is necessary in the interest of democracy, which is always endangered by the concentration of economic power in a few hands, whether the persons exercising it are nominated by a Minister or not. Nationalisation of monopolies is frequently desirable, but it is not desirable that nationalisation should be an instrument for increasing monopolisation.

Finally there is nationalisation as an administrative technique to facilitate some control not itself necessarily connected with the industry nationalised. For example taxes are easiest to collect when the goods taxed pass at some point through the hands of a small number of people, and most difficult to collect when there are many producers selling direct to many consumers without the intervention of a concentrated middleman channel. A government determined to tax, in such a case, may give itself a monopoly of compulsory wholesaling. There are many circumstances in which a government may find it useful to have a monopoly of wholesaling, or, if not a monopoly, at least a substantial share; e.g. in foreign trade, to give effect to bulk contracts, either of purchase or of sale, or to control closely either the quantity or the price or the source or direction of imports or of exports; or in home trade, to be able to promote standardisation by giving bulk orders. To control the wholesale trade is frequently one of the most effective ways of controlling an industry.

Nationalisation, then, is frequently desirable. There is no case for nationalising the whole economy. For nationalisation, when all is said, remains a form of monopoly, subject to all the usual disadvantages of monopoly. It is an improvement on private monopoly and desirable in industries that would in any case be monopolistic, but complete nationalisation should never be introduced in any industry which is not naturally or desirably monopolistic. The reasons for this are the usual reasons against monopoly; that it breeds inefficiency, stifles initiative and concentrates power. A country which depends on its export trade depends on being in the forefront with trying out new ideas, and cannot afford to create any kind of monopoly that is not necessary. And a country whose people love freedom will not wish the state to become the sole employer, through giant corporations. We must have some nationalisation, much more than we have already got (the most obvious candidates for future nationalisation have been mentioned in italics), but we must take each case on its merits, and know where to draw the line.

CONTROL

And when we do nationalise an industry and make it into a monopoly we need to provide for it as great a machinery of control as private monopolies require.

Long experience of public utility control points the way. First, there must be a tribunal with general control over prices charged and services offered to which customers can appeal, as to the old Railway Rates Tribunal and Railway and Canal Commission; every nationalised industry should have its tribunal (it is, for example, a serious omission from the nationalised coal industry). A further corollary of this is a price policy. Nationalised industries must pay their way, on a non-discriminatory basis, and must not be used either as a means of taxation, or as a means of subsidising favoured groups, however deserving; all this should be written into their statutes.

Next a consumers' council is useful, to watch over the interests of consumers, to bargain with the corporation, and to take to the tribunal general issues affecting not just a particular customer but customers as a group, e.g. the general level of prices. A most important function of such a council, also, is to keep an eye on efficiency. Every public corporation should be made to publish detailed information about its costs (as the coal industry does, but not railways or electricity) so that the public may compare its costs with those of similar undertakings in other countries, and compare its parts one with another.

The responsibility for the conditions of the workers, and for seeing that the fullest opportunities are given for participation in management, for promotion, etc., falls upon the appropriate trade unions, whose rights in these spheres need to be specifically recorded in the corporation's charter. If the unions are not satisfied they will, of course, go to arbitration on matters of conditions, or report to the appropriate Minister.

The Minister and Parliament are both last and least in the machinery of control. They cannot be a substitute for the patient and detailed work that has to be done by a price tribunal, by a consumers' council, and by an arbitration board. Ministers should exercise very little control over corporations. Prices, services and conditions of labour are matters for special tribunals. Efficiency and good relations with workpeople are matters that he must review, either independently or at the instance of a consumers' council or of a trade union, since on them depends his judgment of the suitability of the directors he has appointed; and capital investment is clearly his concern. Once a year he should present to Parliament the report of the corporation, with the reports of the tribunal and the consumers' council, and a report from the Ministry of Labour on labour relations, and this should be almost the only occasion on which members of Parliament discuss the corporation's affairs. It will certainly be the only occasion that they have both the time and the relevant material to discuss them intelligently.

CONCLUSION

We may summarise as follows:

(1) Nationalisation is a form of monopoly. Partial nationalisation of industries is useful both as a check on private enterprise and as an outlet for experiment, and may be used widely, but complete nationalisation should be applied only where it is desirable to have a monopoly.

(2) A monopoly should be created wherever efficiency would be increased by bringing an industry under unitary control.

(3) Important monopolies, whether state-created or not, should be nationalised.

(4) The public sector of an industry should be decentralised as much as possible; several public corporations are better than one, except where there are special advantages in unitary control.

(5) In some cases government monopolisation of wholesale trade facilitates desirable economic planning.

(6) Nationalised monopolies should be controlled as closely as any others. Ministers and Parliament cannot achieve much. There should be a price and services tribunal, with a price policy laid down by law, a consumers' council, with access to cost accounts, and the usual machinery for labour arbitration.

IX

How to Plan

so far we have confined ourselves to governmental planning of that part of the economic system which is traditionally the sphere of private enterprise. Beyond this there is, of course, the traditional sphere of public enterprise, which even in the most *laisser-faire* country now usually absorbs about 20 per cent of the national income. We shall not discuss this sphere of planning because the need for such planning and its broad nature are beyond controversy. Everyone agrees that each government department has to decide what it is trying to do, and how and when it intends to do it, and this is all that planning involves —for education, defence, conservation of natural resources, town and country planning, the network of communications —for everything for which the government is responsible it must have a plan of its objectives.

Where planning the private sector and planning the public sector meet is that they both make claims on the national resources, and have therefore to be fitted into the budget for the whole economy.

This is the first stage of planning; on the one hand to estimate the amount of the national income at full employment, and on the other to fit into it the various calls for consumption, investment and public expenditure. In a democratic society the first of these items, consumption, is only to a limited extent within control; it can be expanded fairly easily, but the public resists attempts to restrict consumption, and though the government can reduce consumption by increasing taxation, it cannot restrict it very much below what people voluntarily wish to consume at full employment. This in turn sets limits to the sum of investment and public expenditure. The government can expand the one very easily at the expense of the other; but it cannot expand both beyond the limits set by the public's insistence on consumption without setting in motion the forces of inflation, and producing disequilibrium in the foreign balance.

The master table in the annual plan is therefore that which estimates the national income for the coming year, and proposes its distribution between consumption, investment and public expenditure. The other tables follow from this, and merely translate it into detail.

The consumption table breaks up the global sum, and shows first how people would like to distribute their expenditure between different commodities and services. It then estimates how much of each of these commodities is likely to be available, from home production, from imports and from stocks, with a view to spotting major shortages and surpluses. The investment plan similarly distinguishes the projects that are to be undertaken; estimates the demands on various raw materials, types of plant, and types of labour; sets these demands against likely availabilities; and spots major surpluses and shortages. From these, four other sets of tables follow; a budget for each industry which seems likely to be in serious disequilibrium, a budget for each raw material that will be in short supply, setting demands against availabilities, a manpower budget, and a foreign trade budget.

These subsidiary budgets—for unbalanced industries, scarce raw materials, manpower and foreign trade—provide the crucial information needed at the second stage of planning, for they show where the gravest shortages will lie, and therefore where action is most needed. This action will be of two kinds. First, there will be action to increase supply; this is the most important kind of action, and the primary justification of planning. The secondary justification, and the second kind of action, which is needed only if supply cannot be expanded sufficiently to meet the demand, is to have some means of allocating the short supply, whether by price, or by quota.

This leads to the third stage in planning which is to estimate the equilibrium that these two types of action will achieve; that is to say, to fix the targets. The word target has recently been brought into disfavour by misuse. A target should not be a statement of what we should like to see achieved; that is the figure for demand, which appears in the tables at the second stage of planning. Neither is it the figure of what will be achieved if no action is taken; that is the figure of availabilities also in the second stage. A target is the figure it is proposed to achieve as a result of the action that is contemplated. It is very important that this figure be estimated without illusions as to what is possible. For at this third stage these targets are used to make final allocations in the budgets for unbalanced industries, scarce raw materials, manpower and foreign trade, and to make the final adjustment to the figure for public expenditure in the master plan, which in turn adjusts the other items in that plan. If the targets are fanciful, the whole plan will be fanciful. And this is as true whether the targets are too large or too small. Planners who promise more than they can perform throw everything out of gear, so that the economy might just as well not be planned at all. On the other side there are the planners who take a pride in being able to claim over-fulfilment of their plans, and who therefore deliberately put forward targets that they know to be too low, or else over-fulfil their targets by robbing other essential industries of labour and materials. These are just as big a nuisance, and make just as much of a mockery of planning. Over-fulfilment is just as much a sign of bad planning as is under-fulfilment.

But, of course, however good one's guess may be, and however well planned the measures for achieving the plans, 100 per cent fulfilment is impossible. Over large items the planners have but small control—the prices of imports, the volume of exports, the output of agriculture—and over others all they can hope to do is to exercise an influence in the right direction. Moreover on many basic questions our information is woefully inadequate. Statistics of the British economy are primitive compared with those relating to the U.S.A. and a considerable improvement in both the quantity and the quality of our statistics is needed if economic policy is to be intelligent and precise. At present the best we can do is to try to exercise an influence in the right direction, but this is of course a very important thing to do, and the fact that the figures proposed are never those that are achieved does not make them any the less useful. The purpose of these figures is to indicate the major problems likely to arise, and to enable us to act consistently as far ahead as we can see. We shall know more tomorrow than we know today, but that is no reason for not trying to be as consistent and as intelligent as possible in what we have to do today.

The real moral is that planning must be flexible. In part this means that the ideal is to revise the plans continuously, but this is an impossible ideal to achieve. We should try to achieve it as much as we can, and no doubt, in the event of major unforeseen changes—a slump, a good harvest or a big change in supply or demand—the relevant budgets will be altered. The budgets, however, are all relevant; they all hang together, and if one is changed the whole lot should be changed, and this is a big job which cannot be done several times a year. This is where planning through the market becomes so far superior to planning by direction. For the market itself is a most flexible instrument. If, for example, efforts to increase supply are over-successful, the price will fall, and these efforts will be automatically counteracted, and the surplus automatically absorbed. The planners are not thereby absolved from changing their plans to meet changing conditions, but the consequences of error and delay are less if they plan through the market than if they plan by direction.

A further corollary is that one cannot plan very far ahead. A five year plan cannot be more than a vague indication of aspirations. The national income in five years' time depends first on what happens to productivity. Before the war productivity in this country increased at a rate of about 3 per cent per annum; today it is below the pre-war level, and no one knows whether in five years' time it will be 10 per cent less than pre-war or 30 per cent above pre-war. How can one plan a national income within limits of error so wide that they can swallow up the whole allocation to investment, or to public expenditure, or to exports, or to any major industry? Again the national income five years from now will depend on the terms of trade and the demand for exports, which may affect the balance of payments 20 per cent either way. One must plan five years ahead all those parts of the economy which need five year plans—afforestation, power stations and so on—and one can usefully plan specific investment projects, but a *general* five year plan for the whole economy is no more than a game. One plans for as far ahead as one can see—and this means that even an annual plan must be subject to review.

The fourth stage in planning, when the targets have been drawn up, is to publish the budgets in which they are embodied, with as much data as the public needs in order to understand and to criticise what the government is trying to do. This needs no argument in a democracy, but is nevertheless most vital if planning is to be not a substitute for democracy but an instrument which the public uses to get what it wants. It is not for the government to decide how much we shall invest, or how large an adverse balance of payments we should plan for, or what is the right order of priorities for allocating steel, any more than it is for the government to decide the provisions of the company law or the right age for leaving school. In all these matters the Government must present its proposals to the public, and final acceptance or rejection must lie with Parliament. It is perfectly true that in practice the public can only criticise; it cannot submit a whole new alternative plan, because all the various parts of a plan must hang together, and a new plan can only be made self-consistent by a team of experts. But this is just as true of Parliamentary control over foreign policy, or defence, or the company law, or the government's own budget. All the provision now made for presenting, debating and controlling the government's budget should in future be made for presenting, debating and controlling the economic plan of which the government's budget is only a part.

The documents presented to the public at this stage should show not only what targets are proposed, but also how the government proposes to achieve them. For the sixth and final stage of planning is actually to put into operation the measures which are to achieve the targets. Neglect of this stage makes all that has gone before a farce. To draw up and publish a list of targets is not to plan; the real planning comes when the government takes action to realise these targets. This action, as we have seen, is of two kinds, action to increase supply and action to reduce demand (or *vice versa* if it is not a shortage but a surplus that is in question). Governments frequently take action to reduce demand, but are not so good at taking action to increase supply. They try to plan by exhortation, making speeches urging people to produce more, or to ask themselves whether the job they are doing is vital, and so on, but in fact have no plans, whether of inducement or of direction, to shift resources into the right places. They are then surprised and hurt, at the end of the year, when their plans have not been fulfilled, and they make still more speeches. Planning by exhortation is not planning.

REVIEW

We may conclude by reviewing the principal shortcomings of economic planning in this country in the past three years.

But first we must set the matter in perspective. It is not the case that bad planning has hindered the recovery of this country, and caused us to fare worse than unplanned countries. For we have not in fact fared worse than unplanned countries; on the contrary we have done as well and better. Production has grown as rapidly since the end of the war in the U.K. as it has in the U.S.A. Compared with pre-war years the U.S.A. has far outstripped us, but this is primarily because there were ten million unemployed in the U.S.A. when war broke out, who have now been absorbed. At the time of writing (mid-1948) industrial production is about 20 per cent above pre-war, and agricultural production still larger. There is no other country in Europe affected by the war that can claim such progress—least of all those that have been pursuing *laisser-faire* policies. We could have planned better; but the suggestion that we would have done better if we had planned less has no more value than the statement that others who have planned less have done better than we have, which is made to support it, and which is patently contrary to the facts.

The first shortcoming has been a failure to get labour correctly distributed between industries. We are producing a lot, but too much of the less essential and too little of the more essential. The acid test of this is the failure year after year to realise the targets set in the manpower budget. The major consequence is not enough of the goods that could fetch good prices abroad, especially coal and textiles; consequently a shortfall of exports, restrictions on imports, and continued rationing. The cause of this failure has been reliance on planning by exhortation, instead of taking positive measures to induce movement into the essential trades, and failing this to fill up by immigration. If a ban were placed on ministerial speeches (which seldom do good and often do harm) ministers would have to ask themselves what positive steps they could take to achieve their targets now that mere talk was ruled out, and the efficiency of our planning would improve beyond recognition.[1]

The second shortcoming has been in foreign trade policy, where we have tried to stabilise both the internal and the external value of the pound simultaneously with disastrous consequences for the terms of trade—the U.K. is the only European country against whom the terms of trade have moved since 1938, and if we now enjoyed the same terms as in 1938 the adverse balance would now be negligible.

The third shortcoming has been the pursuit of an inflationary policy, which has raised profits, strained price and raw material controls, dissipated stocks, impeded production, made it difficult to get labour for essential trades, and drawn heavily on our reserves of foreign exchange. The complaint of excessive restrictions, licences, forms and so on has largely followed from this. Inflation puts such a strain on the price mechanism that it becomes necessary to pile on more and more restrictive controls. Happily this phase is now over.

No government can be perfect. There are many other planning errors that have been made, such as slowness in taking steps to increase the productivity of private enterprise, failure to reform the income tax and to impose a capital levy, the passing of inadequate legislation for monopoly control, and the absence of adequate safeguards of the public interest in nationalised industries; but at the present moment these are minor in comparison with the three major errors. That the Government should have made just these errors is a natural outcome of the history of the Labour Party. To socialists in the past, planning has been concerned principally with the distribution of income and with the nationalisation of industry; that is to say principally

---

[1] This paragraph was written in mid-1948. Publication of the *Economic Survey for 1949* while this book was in proof has shown that Ministers have reacted in exactly the opposite way to that suggested above. Having found that targets cannot be hit simply by exhortation, they have now ceased to set targets. Where there are shortages the only 'planning' that is to be done is to ration demand, and even the pretence of planning to eliminate shortages is now dropped. The fact that we still have a lopsided economy is admitted, and also the fact that this lopsidedness costs us dearly in shortages of essential commodities. But the effort to get our resources properly distributed is nevertheless abandoned. Even anti-planners have been shocked by this abdication of an important duty.

It is also to be noted that the budgets for commodities which are still in short supply and still rationed have not been published, so that the public may see, discuss and criticise the basis on which allocations are made. This violates the important principle that planning must be open if it is to be democratic.

with the subject matter of our chapters II and VIII and not with the subject matter of the intervening chapters. Socialist planning has had no principles for dealing with money, investment, foreign trade, mobility, or private enterprise. It is therefore natural that a Labour Government should devote itself with gusto to the subject matter of Chapters II and VIII, and should flounder rather helplessly with everything else. Unfortunately for the government, the standard of living of the workers is much more intimately affected by these other matters; they ought to have a much greater priority in socialist planning than either income distribution or nationalisation, and the fact that a Labour Government always neglects them (exactly the same thing happened in 1929-31) is a tragedy both for the country and for Labour Governments, who are always defeated by just those economic matters that they neglect. Time spent in 1945-47 proudly nationalising the Bank of England, Cable and Wireless, civil aviation or the railways (all desirable measures in themselves) would have been much better devoted to getting labour into the right industries, or to working out policies that would conserve our foreign reserves, for in the hierarchy of planning these are clearly of incomparably greater importance. The greatest lessons that planners have to learn are that nationalisation and the distribution of income are only a small part of the matters that claim their attention; and that when we cannot do everything we must put first things first.

Appendix I

On Economic Union

ECONOMIC union between adjacent countries is widely canvassed today for two reasons. The first is to facilitate discrimination against the United States of America and its deflationary export surplus. Such discrimination, as we have seen, is very desirable, but economic union is rather a big project to use in order to achieve it. The simplest way to bring about this discrimination is for nations to make a joint demand on the United States to appreciate the dollar; or alternatively to effect a joint depreciation of non-dollar currencies. Or discrimination can be effected simply by agreeing to cut dollar imports as much as possible, while relaxing controls on imports from non-dollar sources.

The more important and permanent case for economic union is that, in reducing obstacles to trade, it widens the market and promotes international specialisation. Opponents of union point out that this is not always advantageous to the countries concerned. For example, suppose that before union A and B buy a certain commodity from C, and that after union between A and B the industry is successfully established in A at the expense of C. If the natural economic advantages are heavily in favour of C, both A and B may be worse off for encouraging the industry to establish in A. This is perfectly true, but is not perhaps very important. For what is probable, in the absence of union, is not that the industry will be confined to C, but that both A and B will try to establish it at home under protection, and, compared with this situation, economic union which confines the protection to a large industry in A, is decidedly superior to the prospect of two smaller industries in A and B, both protected. Moreover, C's advantage frequently consists in nothing more than that C has a large market free of trade barriers, and if union does the same for A and B this 'unnatural' advantage disappears. There can be little doubt that if the trade barriers between European countries were removed, all Europe would benefit immensely from the resulting stimulus to specialisation.

It must be emphasised that it is greater specialisation that is the principal benefit. Some people, for example, argue for union on the ground that it will permit greater 'coordination' of industries, by which they mean increased cartelisation. For example every European country is trying to have its own motor car industry, and this is clearly wasteful because the advantages of large scale operation in this industry are immense. If coordination means sharing out the market between the various national industries, through some form of international cartel, the effect will be pernicious. What we really need is that most of these national industries should be swept away, and the whole European market opened up to the product of a very small number of manufacturing centres.

Here lies the rub. Economic union is very difficult to bring about because it is bound to sweep away a great many national practices to which people cling. Let us consider the difficulties systematically.

First of all, what do we mean by economic union? The term covers many degrees of cooperation, and is very loosely used. The minimum requirement is that the currencies of the union should be freely interchangeable without restriction or licence; this does not itself imply union—it was the 'normal' relation between currencies for over a century—but it is the first step. Secondly the decision to free currencies is nullified if at the same time other trade barriers are raised, such as tariffs, or import quotas. The minimum requirement is an undertaking not to increase such barriers, and the union begins to have substance only if there is an undertaking to remove barriers, either immediately or in gradual but pre-determined stages.

When the union comes into effect two sets of problems at once emerge; those that affect particular industries and those that relate to trade in general.

Industries are affected because they lose their protection, or because the removal of barriers in other countries widens their markets. Omelettes cannot be made without breaking eggs, and increased specialisation cannot be achieved without destroying some existing trades. Governments must therefore be ready with plans to move resources out of distressed industries to those that may now expand (including plans to move skilled workmen from one country to another, if this is desirable and if they want to go). But they must turn a deaf ear to suggestions for protection, or the union cannot come into existence. On the other hand they must be ready to remove artificial restraints or subsidies which they themselves have imposed. For example, if there is free trade between Britain and France there cannot be heavy excise duties on beer in Britain but not in France, or British brewers will take their industry to France. This means that all countries in the union must have the same structure of indirect taxation, and of subsidies to industries; union is not just a matter of currencies and tariffs.

The fact that the union destroys some industries is tolerable because it also expands others. But it does this only if it stimulates exports as much as imports, i.e. only if it does not lead to unbalanced trade. For example, if Britain and France now entered into union, Britain would have a heavy export surplus to France, and many French industries would be wiped out while very few would expand. This is because French prices are much higher than British prices. The next step towards union is therefore to bring the price levels of the countries concerned into line with each other. This is not difficult; we have only to find the right rate of exchange between currencies and to establish this rate before the union commences.

The great problem is then to keep the price levels in line in the future. A union cannot last long if one country is trying to stabilise prices and wages, like the U.K., while another is inflating, like France, and a third pursuing a deflationary policy, like Italy. Therefore economic union involves at least an agreement between all the countries concerned to pursue the same policy with respect to money, prices, wages, investment, and employment; and since it is difficult to carry out such an agreement, the logical end of economic union is to have a single government responsible for such matters.

The exception which proves this rule is the working of the sterling pool. Here we have a group of freely interchangeable currencies, without specific agreement to pursue a common economic policy, and indeed without any real similarity of policy. But in the first place the sterling group is not a full economic union. Each partner is free to adopt, and does adopt, measures that partly nullify the free convertibility. Thus British farmers are not overwhelmed by cheap produce from the dominions because the United Kingdom does not permit unrestricted entry of produce even from countries within the sterling group; and free convertibility of currencies does not carry us far when the physical movement of goods is otherwise restrained. And in the second place, even with these restrictions the existence of free convertibility gives rise to problems that are solved only because the political ties existing between the members of the group permit much give and take. Three of these problems are outstanding. First, because sterling is inconvertible, several members of the group receive in return for their exports only an addition to their holdings of sterling, just as in economic union with France we would receive for exports a large holding of inconvertible francs; in the case of the sterling group, members are willing to hold sterling without complaint because of their affection for the United Kingdom, but in the case of economic union we should not be so willing to send exports to France in return for a holding of francs. Secondly, each member agrees to pool its dollar earnings, and the Treasury is allowed, in consultation, to determine how many dollars each member may spend. Malaya surrenders dollars to the sterling pool, and the United Kingdom also makes substantial contributions (proceeding from loans) for the benefit of other members of the group. Belgium might not feel so generous to other members of an economic union. Nevertheless it is essential in such a union that earnings of non-union currencies be pooled. Otherwise each country has the incentive to withhold its goods from union members and to direct its exports as much as possible say to dollar countries, thus frustrating the free movement of goods intended by the union. And thirdly, even in the sterling area movements of capital from one member to another give rise to anxieties, and are carefully watched. These difficulties are overcome in the sterling group because the members are prepared, because of their common membership of the Empire, to accept some sacrifice; and those members of the Empire which cannot afford the drain that would otherwise be upon them stay out of the group. In an economic union of Western Europe the difficulties would be even more acute, because the economies of the countries are much more competitive (the sterling group countries are more complementary), and would therefore more urgently have to pursue similar economic policies; while on the other hand the will to give and take, which smoothes the working of the sterling area, would not be so pronounced.

It would be virtually impossible to carry on an economic union in Western Europe without having a political union with a central government responsible for economic policy. This is not a strange conclusion when we remember the problems presented by local authorities within a unitary state, or by state governments within a federation. If local authorities were free to pursue conflicting monetary policies a country would soon be in a mess. We recognise as an elementary principle of political economy, that if there is to be free movement of men, money and goods inside a country, whether unitary or federal, then there must be severe limits on the economic powers of subordinate authorities. We apply this principle even to the provision of social services. If one area has elaborate services and high taxes, while others have fewer services and smaller taxes, business is driven from the high to the low tax area, and this will be true whether the areas are Yorkshire and Lancashire, Pennsylvania and Illinois, or England and France. An economic union, in fact, will not long work smoothly unless it becomes a political federation, with the more important economic functions of government transferred from the state to the federal authority.

Now it is a pre-condition for this further stage that countries should agree broadly to pursue similar economic policies. A union between *laisser-faire* peoples is easy to achieve, because each of the peoples knows that the federal authority will pursue the same sort of economic policy that its own national government would have pursued. But a people that favours planning cannot live in the same federation with a people that favours *laisser-faire*. And even the peoples that favour planning cannot agree on a federation unless the types of planning that they favour are broadly similar.

The great obstacle to plans for economic union in Western Europe is the unplanned and unstable economy of France. So long as France continues to abandon herself to inflation all other countries have to protect their economies against her, and there is not much hope of barriers coming down. But if France can pull herself together, and establish a strong administration, the main obstacle to economic union will fall away. For the principal countries of Western Europe have now all abandoned *laisser-faire* (all their political parties agree on this), and it would not be impossible (though it would not be easy) to reach agreement on the general lines of economic policy, and even to surrender some crucial economic powers to a federal authority. Or it may be, on the other hand, that participation in economic union is just what France needs to ensure a sound economic policy.

In the last analysis the success of economic union depends on the strength with which political union is desired. The difficulties are formidable, but once it comes to be realised that the very continuance of democracy in Western Europe depends on the nations finding military and political strength in unity, the economic obstacles will be seen to be of little importance.

Appendix II

On Planning in Backward Countries

PLANNING is at the same time much more necessary and much more difficult to execute in backward than in advanced countries.

In the first place, planning requires a strong, competent and incorrupt administration. It must be strong enough to be able to enforce its measures, such as to collect taxes from the peasantry, or to enforce a rationing system without black markets, measures which even so ancient a government as that of France has not found itself fully able to enforce. It must have a competent administrative service, with trained personnel, able to understand the large issues that are at stake, and to act reasonably and rapidly. And it must be free of all charge of corruption, since, whereas men will bear many restrictions from a government which they believe to be acting fairly and solely in the public interest (however mistakenly) without respect of persons, they will sooner or later resist violently measures which are corruptly administered, however acceptable the measures themselves may be.

Now a strong, competent and incorrupt administration is just what no backward country possesses, and in the absence of such an administration it is often much better that governments should be *laisser-faire* than that they should pretend to plan. This was indeed the essence of the case for *laisser-faire* made by eighteenth century writers, who saw the mess that was made by weak, incompetent and corrupt governments, and sought therefore to confine the activities of government within the narrowest practicable limits, so as to minimise the damage that they might do. The alternative approach was that of Lenin, who fully realised the impossibility of using a backward administrative service for planning, and who sought therefore to create, in his Communist Party, a highly trained and disciplined priestly order, on which he could rely to carry out his instructions.

At least we may say this: the first objective of planners must be to create an administrative machine that can do the work of planning; to train young men academically and in the tasks of administration, and to weed out mercilessly the incompetent and the corrupt. And, secondly, in the meantime no administration should be loaded with tasks more numerous or more delicate than it can handle; the quantity and forms of planning should be limited strictly within the capacity of the machine.

In backward countries governments have usually much leeway to make up in fulfilling the normally accepted functions of governments long before they get on to more controversial matters. The usual public works are usually in a deplorable state. Roads and communications have to be planned; rivers to be brought under control, to put an end to flooding, and utilised for irrigation and electric power; water supplies must be conserved, and pipes laid to bring water to reasonably accessible places; elementary public health measures are wanting, the draining of swamps, the control of infectious disease, the regulation of sanitation, the establishment of a public health service. Forests, schools, geological research, hospitals, courts, police—one could continue this list at length. City dwellers in Western Europe or the U.S.A. take for granted a vast network of government services which are absent or grossly inadequate in backward countries, and which it is the recognised first duty of governments to provide.

But the difficulty which faces these governments is that they cannot expand their own services unless they can raise money to pay for them, and they cannot raise all the money they need because their peoples are too poor. They are therefore driven to concern themselves with measures to increase the national income. This is the sense in which planning is more necessary in backward countries. In advanced countries the national income increases steadily from decade to decade even if the government does not 'interfere' in economic life. But in many backward countries there is either stagnation or retrogression, and a progressive government is naturally driven to enquire what plans it may make to bring about economic progress.

The crux of the problem is usually a backward system of agriculture—lack of scientific knowledge, poor equipment, inefficient marketing, insecure tenure, an uneconomically small scale of operation, and, frequently also, rural overpopulation. There are recognised remedies—an agricultural extension service, cooperative and other provision of credit, cooperative and other reorganisation of marketing, legislation to protect the security of tenants—but they make little headway unless the interest and enthusiasm of the farmers is awakened and held. Once the farmers begin to desire progress almost all difficulties can be overcome, but so long as they are apathetic and uninterested very little can be done. The first task of progressive governments in the sphere of agriculture is to arouse the enthusiasm of their people for new knowledge and new ways of life. How to awaken and capture enthusiasm is the first problem in mass education. It is also politically the first task of new popular governments, and it is because only new popular governments can capture such enthusiasm that it is only in the countries which have had such governments that there has been substantial progress in agriculture among backward peoples in the last thirty years.

The most difficult of all the agricultural problems is the small size of holdings in peasant countries, frequently of five acres or less. All such countries have to go through an agrarian revolution at the end of which is some form of large scale agriculture, whether it be the capitalist farm, or the collective farm, or the state farm, or merely the family farm, working large areas with machinery but without hired labour. In the past an agrarian revolution has always been violent, even where, as in England, the violence may have been cloaked in Parliamentary forms. It remains to be seen whether popular governments can awaken sufficient enthusiasm for their mass education programmes to carry through such revolutions in future by consent. So far the omens are unfavourable. Popular revolutions have just the opposite result. Large estates are broken up into small uneconomic holdings sometimes not exceeding five acres, with disastrous effects on productivity. Techniques for combining democracy with large scale agriculture have still to be worked out.

Large scale agriculture usually requires fewer people per acre than small holdings, and therefore where the countryside is overpopulated and there are not enough new lands reclaimable by drainage or irrigation, it is not desirable to make an agrarian revolution without providing new employment opportunities outside agriculture. An agricultural and an industrial revolution always go together, the first releasing the labour which the second draws off the land. Governments of backward countries have therefore to put into their agricultural programmes projects for industrialisation.

Since this problem is one of disguised unemployment it is sometimes suggested (for example by implication in the Bombay plan for India) that it can be solved, as is unemployment in industrial countries, simply by increasing the quantity of money. But this is not so. Suppose that the government starts to build roads, and creates the money to pay wages and salaries. In the first place, the propensity to import is very high; much of this money goes abroad to import food, clothes, bicycles and so on. There is then a strain on the balance of payments unless exports can be increased correspondingly, but this is not easy, and cannot be achieved even by devaluation. If it were achieved, the quantity of goods on the home market would be correspondingly reduced—the extra imports go to receivers of the new incomes, but receivers of old incomes have now to yield up part of the old produce to these same people and part for export, and so there is inflation created at home. The situation is then the same as if the government controlled imports and did not allow the new money to be spent abroad. This, in practice, is what it has to do; control of the exchanges is one of the first things planners have to do in backward countries because they are not able to expand exports adequately in view of their high propensity to import.

Control of the exchanges does not, however, solve the problem; the new money then circulates at home and forces prices up. In an industrial country this would cause entrepreneurs to take on labour, and output would expand rapidly. But in an agricultural country as likely as not when prices rise the farmers begin by consuming more of their own produce, thus reducing the amount available to the towns and raising prices still further. They next go to the towns with their extra money to buy imported goods, and on finding that these are now in short supply (because the circulation of new money has increased the demand but not the supply) they may return home and reduce their sowings. This, for example, is what happened in Russia until agriculture was collectivised, and was one of the chief reasons why the Government was so anxious to bring the farms under its control. In an industrial country an increase in the quantity of money increases employment and output, but in an agricultural country, even when there is unemployment, open or disguised, an increase in the quantity of money frequently reduces output.

It follows that if governments of backward countries try to finance their investments by creating money they will cause inflation. Investment must be financed either by taxation, or by borrowing. In very backward countries the propensity to import is almost unity; that is, almost all extra income is spent on imports, and even local borrowing cannot finance investment unless the lenders either lend out of foreign reserves, or reduce their own demands on imports to the full extent of the propensity to import.

It also follows that more positive steps are needed than the mere creation of money if the unemployed are to be absorbed in productive enterprise. In an industrial country there are entrepreneurs eager to respond to the prospects of increased profits by installing new industrial enterprises and engaging workers. But in an agricultural country the enterprise and experience are confined to agriculture and to commerce. Moreover, because the 'external economies' are large in industrial production, small isolated factories seldom pay, and entrepreneurs will not easily establish in new areas when they have a choice of old areas already well supplied with cheap power laid on, with trained industrial labour, with information services, and with all the other accessories of a developed industrial centre. In these days if one wishes to develop secondary industries, one must do it on a large scale, and deliberately set out to create the facilities which factories use in common, and which cannot be provided cheaply on a small scale. That is why the trading estate, financed by government, is now the established technique for developing depressed areas. And it is also why, once an area has started to decline, it tends to decline cumulatively; and once it has started to expand, it tends also to expand cumulatively. Any backward country which wishes to encourage industrialisation—and they nearly all must if only as a part of their agricultural programme—must, as a minimum, set about building a trading estate, and offering inducements to industrial entrepreneurs to set up in its territory.

Foreign capital cannot be avoided, even if the government decides to build and operate all the plants itself. The machinery must come from abroad, and the workers who build the factories, the roads, the factory workers' houses and so on will want to spend a large part of their wages on imported goods. Some foreign exchange can be found by using a strict exchange control to cut out all luxury imports, and to pare down even necessaries; and by using what is thus saved to buy machinery. (There must be corresponding taxation or borrowing to mop up the incomes thus diverted to the home market, in order to prevent inflation.) But backward countries are too poor to be able to provide much capital simply by cutting down luxuries. If they are to industrialise substantially they have either to cut severely into the consumption of necessaries, or else to borrow abroad. A ruthless dictatorship can cut consumption to the desired extent, but a democracy will always have to rely largely on foreign capital in its early stages of development.

The quickest way to ease the strain on the foreign exchanges, and to reduce the dependence on foreign borrowing, is to plan the new investment in such a way that its produce becomes rapidly available, and adds to exports or can be substituted for imports. Export industries have first priority. Next comes food. In most backward countries output is low partly because people are undernourished or malnourished. Investments which increase the output of food, such as by irrigation, or reclaiming lands, or increasing manuring or livestock, are of the greatest urgency, especially if they are such as to yield their results rapidly. There is also a high propensity to import food, so such investments quickly reduce the strain on foreign reserves. Then there are the clothing industries and building materials, which also have a high import propensity. Weaving, knitting and the making of clothes and of boots and shoes are simple industrial processes, and are always among the first to be developed. Building materials depend on the existence of suitable local earths and forests; where these are available they should be rapidly exploited.

Now industry cannot flourish if there are no industrial resources whatever in the territory—especially if there is no source whatever of power—and however overcrowded an area may be, if it has no industrial resources it must seek other sources of employment—a tourist industry, a film industry, or failing all else employment in other lands that permit migration. Industry depends also on a sizeable home market. There are many areas that are very overcrowded, but which nevertheless have too small a total population to be able to support industry. The world will get into a mess if each small backward political unit embarks upon industrialisation. The remedy for most of these units is political and economic federation, which, by widening the market, increases specialisation, and makes it possible to develop economically.

There are also backward countries whose problem is not overpopulation but under-population, perhaps the classical example being the colony of Northern Rhodesia whose population of one and a half million is dispersed over an area three times the size of Great Britain. In such countries the problem is rather that of husbanding one's resources. To build roads, schools, waterworks and other capital goods all over the country would be much too costly. One must start in small areas, encourage the population to concentrate there, and move outward only as numbers increase. How to plan new settlements systematically is a subject as old as Gibbon Wakefield, and one in which new techniques have been developed in recent years, especially by the Dutch in the out islands of the former Netherlands East Indies. The problems here are quite different from those of the overpopulated backward areas.

It can thus be seen that planning in backward countries imposes much bigger tasks on governments than does planning in advanced countries. The government has to do many things which can in advanced countries be left to entrepreneurs. It has to create industrial centres, to put through an agricultural revolution, to control the foreign exchanges most strictly, and in addition to make up a great leeway of public services and of ordinary economic legislation. And all this has to be done through a civil service that is usually much inferior to that of an advanced country. Why then do backward countries take more readily to planning? Because their need is also so obviously much greater. And it is also this that enables them to carry it through in spite of error and incompetence. For, if the people are on their side, nationalistic, conscious of their backwardness, and anxious to progress, they willingly bear great hardships and tolerate many mistakes, and they throw themselves with enthusiasm into the job of regenerating their country. Popular enthusiasm is both the lubricating oil of planning, and the petrol of economic development—a dynamic force that almost makes all things possible. We in the United Kingdom felt this during the war, and can understand the claims of Russia in the 1930s or of Jugoslavia today to have awakened this dynamic enthusiasm and to be conquering all things with it. Even the most backward country will progress rapidly if its government knows how to tap this dynamic force.